D0996620

A NATURALIST
ON SPEYSIDE

A NATURALIST ON SPEYSIDE

by
Henry Tegner

1971
GEOFFREY BLES
LONDON

SBN: 7138 0294 4

Printed in Great Britain
by Richard Clay (The Chaucer Press), Ltd.
Bungay, Suffolk

Published by
GEOFFREY BLES LTD
52 Doughty Street, London, WCIN 2LZ
36–38 Clarence Street, Sydney, N.S.W. 2000
353 Elizabeth Street, Melbourne, C.1
246 Queen Street, Brisbane
CML Building, King William Street, Adelaide, S.A. 5000
Lake Road, Northcote, Auckland
100 Lesmill Road, Don Mills, Ontario
P.O. Box 8879, Johannesburg
P.O. Box 834, Cape Town
P.O. Box 2800, Salisbury, Rhodesia

Contents

Illustrations

Illustrations

CHAPTER I

Great River

In the grey mountains of the Monadhliath range, within the country of Inverness-shire, lies the deer forest of Corrieyairack. Here, amongst the peat and heather of this high tundra land, is the little loch of Spey. This is the source of the lovely river of the same name which flows through Badenoch and the broad Strath of Spey into the North Sea at Port Gordon. Spey travels through the greater part of the breadth of Scotland, and seldom, in its course, does it pass through a countryside which is not beautiful. During the past half-century it has been my good fortune to have been able to spend much of my leisure time in this part of Scotland. It can be exciting country to the botanist, geologist, ornithologist and, in fact, anyone at all interested in natural history.

In the corries and great glens, through which Spey runs, are contained most specimens of our British wild fauna. Spey's bird-life is prolific, and it can claim, in the primeval forests of Rothiemurchus and Abernethy, through parts of which the river travels, the rare crested tit found nowhere else in the British Isles. Why this active little bird with its shrill, high-pitched squeak should favour only the shelter of Spey's woodlands no one really seems to know.

Nearly all the curved-billed, claw-footed British birds of prey are represented within this realm. The golden eagle soars above Corrieyairack and the Cairn Gorms—more of a carrion bird than a killer-falcon; he is on the increase again in Scotland, where there is much fat living for him in the dead red deer, occasional stricken sheep, live blue hares, ptarmigan and red grouse, which are all to be found amongst the neighbouring high hills. Where the young river Spey joins the Mashie

9

Water it meets the main road which, for a considerable distance, travels alongside the river through Newtonmore, Kingussie, Kingcraig and Aviemore to grey Grantown-on-Spey.

Along this road the buzzard hunts in search of the lesser birds and beasts which have succumbed to man's modern fast-moving traffic. The swift peregrine falcon, with its odd pigeon-like flight, nests in various selected sites in the valley. The vertical face behind the modern tower-like Strathspey Hotel at Aviemore is a regular eyrie of the peregrine. This site is within the minute Craigellachie National Nature Reserve which consists of about a square mile of birch woodlands overlooking Aviemore.

The sparrow hawk, and certainly the kestrel, are common enough throughout the long Strath of Spey; and the little merlin can occasionally be observed skimming the hills in its swallow-like flight. The merlin, the smallest of all the British hawks, was once named "the lady's hawk" because the bird would sit so lightly on its mistress's hand.

The great capercaillie, known in the past as the giant grouse, is well-established in many of the mature woodlands along the river from Fochabers to Newtonmore; in the spring the big cock bird's fantastic nuptial display, as he courts his hen in the light of dawn, is a sight which, once witnessed, is never likely to be forgotten.

From the mountain birds like the snow-buntings, dotterels and ptarmigan to the riverine waders such as the oyster-catchers, redshanks and sandpipers they are all here, somewhere, along the length of Spey. The snowy owl, which in 1967 successfully hatched out a clutch in Fetlar in Shetland, visited the slopes above Loch Morlich in 1966. A friend of mine, Hamish Marshall of Grantown-on-Spey, a most reliable observer, saw the bird one weekend, and succeeded in getting quite close up to it as it sat perched on a rock, looking for all the world like some little snow-man, as he so aptly described it.

The largest of the British birds, the huge whooper swan, and the smallest, the gold-crest, are both at times residents. Grey geese travel along the river's course in their migrations north-eastwards in the spring and south-westwards in the fall.

A very considerable number of the wild animals of Britain are to be found within the glens, corries, moorlands and culti-vated areas through which the river twists and turns.

In the mountains where Spey has its source you will find the blue, or mountain hare, whilst lower down in its fast-flowing waters the melanistic water vole, once considered almost an exclusive Scottish species, may be glimpsed swimming towards its retreat along the river's banks. Spey has its full quota of the swimming mammalian predators, from the sleek, lovely otter to the immigrant mink; now unfortunately feral on certain stretches. The emancipated mink is so much of a natural water-lover as to be named "the fisher" in its native land of America. The indigenous red deer, *Cervus elaphus scoticus*, and the roe-deer, *Capreolus capreolus*, are very numerous in the hills and woods. The foreign fallow deer, *Dama dama*, used to be found in the woods by Arndilly and Craigellachie, but whether they still survive I am not sure. They were certainly there in the early half of the present century, for I used to see some occa-sionally in the dawn along the fringes of the woodlands above Spey's banks. Probably the greatest concentration of this foreign species in Scotland today is to be found farther south on Tay-side by Dunkeld.

Reindeer once roamed the Strath of Spey—this we know from the discovery of fossilised remains in the district—but they became extinct in this area before the twelfth century, together with other indigenous Scottish cervine species such as the moose. The horn of a young moose, found in a peat hag, was sent to me from Speyside not long ago; it is a fragile specimen, and it now resides in Kenneth Whitehead's inter-nationally known deer museum in Cheshire.

Today reindeer roam about the Cairn Gorm ski-lifts; their reintroduction to the Scottish scene is dealt with in a separate chapter. The fox, the badger, the wild cat, and perhaps the pine marten, are local inhabitants. Both the pine marten, which was once common on nearby Laggan-side, and the wild cat almost reached extinction point during the latter part of the last century, but today both species would appear to be on the increase. However, the wild cat and the pine marten, together with the otter, are amongst our most secretive creatures, and they are very difficult indeed to see.

Wild goats may occasionally be seen grazing within sight of the railway, which runs parallel with Spey for so much of its course, by Lethendry Voil which is a few miles north of Aviemore and close to Kinveachy, one of the many properties of Lord Seafield. For the naturalist, botanist and bird-watcher Spey offers much, and it would hardly be an exaggeration to say that there are few places in Britain today capable of providing the wide variety of exciting fauna and flora which is contained within this long, wide, lovely strath.

The spring of the year is as good a time as any to see the wild birds and beasts. Vegetation is low in early May, which makes for easy observation. Many of the immigrant birds have arrived or are arriving. Last year spring came late to the valley. June still saw extensive snowfields on the upper ranges of the Cairn Gorm hills. Wild hyacinths and primroses were in full bloom in the middle of the month. Many of the deciduous trees were still only scantily clothed in leaves at the end of June. For weeks there was little rain, and the burns dried up so that one could walk across them dryshod; yet Spey itself, strangely, fished well for salmon. This surprised many anglers who were convinced that regular spates were necessary to keep the fish moving.

The low state of the river had exposed its extensive beaches of stone and shingle. The riverine birds nested well, for no floods took their toll of the waders' nests. The glens appeared to pullulate with life. Oyster-catchers, with their brilliant orange-yellow beaks and their distinctive black-and-white plumage, were everywhere. Their strident whistling echoed over the riverside fields in company with the mellower call of the dun-coloured, curved-billed curlews.

The adult peewits with their proud, upstanding, feathered crests were busy looking after their still flightless young; quick runners the little ones but inadequate aerobats as yet, they appeared well-grown compared with the downy infant curlews. The loss of baby life, through spate and storm, had obviously been low. The defensive tactics of the parent plovers and curlews were interesting to observe. The peewits would call at the approach of man or dog to start an aerial dance of diversion, trying by such means to draw the intruder's attention away from their chicks to themselves. The curlews appeared to prefer concealing tactics. They would freeze when they could scarcely be distinguished from a stone or a heap of dung. The curlew chicks seemed to have an instinctive knowledge of concealment. Whilst watching three young curlews with their parents one afternoon by Dulnain Bridge, I saw a hen harrier quartering the vale like some great, silent owl. All the curlews quietened and then seemed to go to ground.

Sandpipers there were in plenty. The exposed stretches of Spey's bed were providing them with abundant feeding. The dry weather seemed to have favoured the snipe as well. It made one wonder whether a wet spring had the same calamitous effect on the nests of these birds and their chicks as it is known to have on those of the other wading species. Somehow the snipe is so essentially a bird of the wet places, that it is difficult to believe that such an event as an excess of water could mean disaster.

The dippers gave one the impression that they rather resented the lack of water. The greater the flush the more they appear to enjoy themselves. In their quick, darting flights amongst the dry stones of the exposed watercourses they looked as if they were constantly on the look-out for a turbulent spate. Never before had I seen so many blackheaded gulls along Spey.

Although much of the bird life of the valley had flourished that spring, there seemed some doubt about the breeding of both the grouse and the local partridges. The grouse, one of

Seafield's keepers told me, had done fairly well on the lower moorlands, but the birds on higher terrain had suffered somewhat from the long-lying, early spring snows. Forest fires, he said, had been serious. The lack of rain and the general dryness of the countryside had made many of the softwood plantations and the heatherlands into frighteningly combustible areas. I was surprised to learn that five out of six fires which had started in the valley during the past ten days, had been caused by railway engines, and not, as I was accustomed to believe, by the rejected cigarette or the picnic fireplace of a careless motorist or thoughtless camper.

"The sparks from an engine's funnel are like a shower of red-hot bricks," said the keeper.

The valley of the Spey is well-timbered. There is much potential tinder. The coming of the diesel and eventually, perhaps, electric trains should certainly result in a lesser risk of fire.

CHAPTER II

Glenmore

It was a day in early May. Snow still lay in the high corries of the Cairn Gorms. The chairlift and the ski-tow were both working. Never having experienced a trip on the chairlift before, I decided to try a ride. Leaving my car in the extensive parking ground I walked with my Jack Russell terrier to the ticket booth. Entering the cold concrete shed, my terrier crouched with fear at the sound of the deep drone of the electric motor as it worked its endless belt of chairs up towards the mountain above.

Mattie had been hit by a car a year previously, and since had been terrified of the sound of an engine, although she shows no fear of my own car, in fact, she appears to love it and, at times, it is difficult to keep her out of it. As soon as I entered the building I realised that I had left Mattie's lead behind in the hotel where I was staying. Outside the power-house of the chairlift I found a piece of rope which I picked up and made into a kind of lead for her.

A middle-aged lady, in a glass kiosk, took my fare for the journey up Cairn Gorm. I was a little surprised that dogs were allowed to accompany passengers on the flimsy-looking open seats. Carrying Mattie in my arms I got on board my chair, and was secured into my seat by a big man who seemed to ooze confidence. He must have had hundreds of cowards through his hands before. The metal bar across my knees seemed a frail protection against falling out. The harsh rumble of machinery set Mattie shivering.

As we emerged from the gloom of the concrete building into the brilliant sunlight of the May day, the scene, spread out on all sides, was overwhelming. The impact of the vast view lasted only a brief while, for we were being hoisted faster and higher along that endless, frail-looking wire above our heads. It was cold in the Highland air, and I was glad of my Barbour oilskin, which I had put on before venturing on my aerial voyage. There was scarcely a puff of wind; and the silence, broken only by the ceaseless murmur of the pulley wheels and the regular jolting bumps which came as the chair passed beneath the pylons, was impressive.

It was almost like being in a glider in flight, except that I have never felt fearful in a flying machine, whilst I dreaded this lift. I found I was getting as nervous as the bundle of twitching flesh in my arms. I began to imagine Mattie panicking and trying to jump overboard. Would she dangle at the end of her rope to die by hanging, or would she dive to her death, hundreds of feet below amongst the litter-strewn snow? My morbid contemplations were quickly ended when the metal chair, in which we had been confined, entered the half-way halt.

I left my seat quickly and walked out into the sunshine, Mattie still tightly clasped in my arms. The rope, tied around her neck, trailed behind us along the ground. For the rest of the way to the summit of Cairn Gorm we walked by the zig-zag track which had been gouged out of the mountainside by some gigantic mechanical plough.

Memories of Glenmore and Cairn Gorm before they became a popular tourist resort, flooded my mind, whilst the broken ground which was the path jarred through the soles of my shoes with its many stones and great boulders of granite. Once past the final lift station I took to the footpath, now deeply grooved by the feet of many a hiker, up to the peak of Cairn Gorm.

The evidence of passing humanity, in the form of litter, was not nearly so pronounced along the footpath as I was to find it on the slopes beside the ski-tow and the chairlift. Coming home down the hillside below the chairlift I made a brief survey of the muck that man had left on the earth's surface. Mufflers, caps, gloves, paper, flags, cartons, bottles, orange

Roedeer are very numerous in the woods

Reindeer once roamed the Strath of Spey

The golden eagle soars above Corrieyarack

and banana skins—it would take a page to contain the list. Much of this material must have fallen from the occupants of the lifts themselves as they travelled overhead; but an equal amount of man's undesirable residue must have been abandoned in full flight by the ski-ing fraternity in their hurtling descent towards the lower slopes of the snowfields.

Glenmore today is certainly the most popular National Park in Scotland. It has both the scope and the various intrinsic attractions to enable it to hold this position. In 1967 the British Ski Championships were held on the Glenmore slopes. This event fortunately was blessed with perfect weather and snow, something which cannot always be guaranteed. It was the first time the Championships were held outside the Swiss Alps, and they proved a considerable success.

When I first knew Glenmore it was one of the more attractive small private sporting estates in Scotland. The variety of game the place provided was unusual. Besides grouse and red deer, there were many roedeer in the natural woods about Loch Morlich and the Lodge. In and around the loch of Morlich and the Green Lochan there were capercaillie, blackgrouse, snipe and various ducks; whilst up on the high-tops, where I was now hiking with Mattie, there were plenty of ptarmigan. There are still a few left, for I sprang a small covey on my way down to the car-park by the footpath to Glenmore Lodge.

The Lodge, which is now a national institution, was a long, white, rambling place full of corridors panelled with planks of varnished pitch-pine. The garden used to contain a great variety of fruits, flowers and vegetables. It was the gardener's proud possession. The last time I saw it, it was but a pale shadow of its original self; weeds reached above a man's head.

Although by no means one of Scotland's larger forests, Glenmore provided as fine deer-stalking as one could wish for. We had a limit of some twenty-four stags and double that number of hinds. There were two professional stalkers on the ground: John Macdonald—always known as John Macdonald of Glenmore—and the second stalker Murdo McKenzie, who eventually became nationalised himself, as he went to the Electricity Board, employed as a shepherd, over on the other side of Scotland.

John Macdonald was a splendid man, well over six feet in his socks. He married comparatively late in life and reared a big family. He also bred some of the best deer ponies in Scotland. Highland garrons, trained by Macdonald to carry deer, fetched very high prices. Now Land-Rovers and motor-caterpillars do the work formerly done by the ponies in the deer forests. John Macdonald also specialised in Gordon setters, a breed of dog one seldom sees on a grouse moor these days; they were, like all of John's animals, trained to perfection. Occasionally we would walk up grouse on the slopes below the present site of the chairlift. Twelve to fifteen brace was no unusual bag. Now a red grouse on this ground is a rarity. The woods around Loch Morlich and behind the Lodge had not then become planted with rows of regimented conifers.

On the odd day off from deer-stalking we would have impromptu drives, or rather they were moves of game in these wild woodlands. Such bye-days always seemed to yield an attractive variety of species. They were odd days, these occasions with the shotgun, in nearly every sense of the word. Standing beneath the cover of an old gnarled Scots fir you never knew what might appear: a great cock caper—once airborne almost as silent in flight as a swallow—or a quick zig-zagging snipe sprung by a beater from the damp ground beside Loch Morlich. It was the old blackcocks who usually provided the best shooting, for by topping the trees with their deceptively slow wing-beats they would pass safely over the guns time and time again. In numbers slain these occasional forays were of little account, but then we were not out for records; we would only shoot for the pot—enough for ourselves and the staff at the Lodge.

In these woodland drives roedeer always came forward to the guns, but they were never fired at for they were preserved for the excellent stalking they could provide. Glenmore, in the past, was certainly one of the best places for the stalking of roebucks in all Scotland. When the Forestry Commission first came on to this property to plant foreign trees, they started off with a policy of total elimination. Every deer of any species, within the planned planting area, was due for slaughter. The roedeer, and to a lesser extent the red deer, suffered severely. In fact it became almost an event to see a roe in this area quite soon after the Forestry Commission entered the ground. Birds, too, were proscribed—the capercaillie and the black grouse were for it, since they were shot all the year round; and any nests found had the heel of a forester into the clutch. The Forestry Commission's policy has changed since their early days at Glenmore, but the damage had been largely done. Glenmore has never really recovered.

After reaching the cairn on Cairn Gorm's summit, in company with a number of other visitors, I turned back downhill for the car-park. I took the track I knew so well of old, now worn almost to the smoothness of a concrete pavement by the feet of innumerable hikers. In the past these moss-strewn flats, at an altitude of over 3,000 feet, were good places for the ptarmigan, a most attractive game bird, with its queer grating voice and its remarkably swift, slithering flight. Shooting these Highland birds was always hard work, for you had to walk up to their level from the Lodge before you started your day's sport. It was well worth it though, because once at that altitude the world about you was particularly your own.

Telling Mattie to sit, I selected a convenient rock to lean against and proceeded to glass the panorama all around me with my binoculars. I found no sign of red deer. Down by the car-park a lone reindeer, with a collar around its neck, was snuffling amongst the litter for some edible matter. Then I heard the sound of flighting geese. A skein of sixty birds came flying in perfect formation, from over the waters of Morlich. Out on the Rothiemurchus march I picked up, in my field-glasses, six red deer; they were not very far from the limits of the old reindeer fence around Silver Hill. There was a small stag in the herd. The deer seemed restive. Something appeared to be disturbing them. Forty human beings, dressed in all the colours of the rainbow, came walking through the woods in a long crocodile. It was too far for me to hear their voices, but they would not be silent, and the red deer were soon on the move. Coming down lower to heather level I searched for signs of red grouse. I never found a single dropping, nor did I see a living sign of *Lagopus scoticus* all day.

Another small lot of geese came overhead; they were not so numerous as the previous skein. The birds were flying low, and they seemed to be only a few hundred feet above my head as they climbed in the sky heading northwards. A laggard bird, rather like a child who will not keep up with the rest, flew last and well below the other birds in their orderly formation—perhaps the laggard had been injured farther south earlier in the year, I wondered. Except for the geese, the small parcel of red deer in Rothiemurchus, and the fleeting glimpse of ptarmigan, I saw little else until I spotted a kestrel hovering over the spruce woods beside Loch Morlich.

When I arrived at the parking place it had filled considerably. There were vehicles of all sorts, beside some of which pressure-stoves were hissing in the open, whilst folding chairs and tables had been brought out by the car owners for their necessary comfort, and odd scraps of paper and empty cellophane packages blew here and there in the slight breeze. It was not difficult to understand why the once plentiful wild-life had departed from Glenmore—for *homo sapiens* had come to take over.

CHAPTER III

Rothiemurchus

The old cart track from Coylumbridge to the head-waters of Loch Einich runs through some of the most beautiful country in Scotland. For a great part of its length the road travels parallel with the sparkling Beinne burn which has its source in the great sweeping corrie of the same name. The Beinne, at times, can become a rushing mountain stream whose waters, after a period of rain, will run black as stout surfaced with brown froth, when the swirling river comes up against great boulders in its course. At other times the Beinne can be particularly benevolent; especially during a long, dry spell when it makes its silent way down towards the Spey. Like so many other Highland streams the mood of Beinne never seems the same on two consecutive days, but somehow she always seems to sparkle be she brown or crystal clear.

Rothiemurchus is within the area of the Cairn Gorm National Nature Reserve, the largest reserve in Britain, being over 100 square miles in extent. It is a changeless place, and there is something basically primeval about it.

It was in the month of June when I last walked up the glen. The day was warm with the sky above a depthless blue. Away to the north tiny, white clouds hung, like wisps of lamb's wool, in the azure ceiling. A soft breeze from the west made good walking weather. The old woods, along the banks of the Beinne burn, were fragrant with the smell of pine. Coming out on to the short stretch of open, heather-clad moorland by Whitewell, I looked for the roedeer which always, in the past, used to haunt the silver-birch woods by the path's side. At least some of their descendants were still there, for I caught a glimpse of two bounding white rump-patches as a pair of animals sprang into the dense juniper bushes beyond the Lairig path. Mattie, being low on the ground, had not spotted their bouncing sterns.

By Achnacoichen, where the Nature Conservancy warden now lives, I hoped to catch a glimpse of blackgame as, at one time, the green hummocks by Achnacoichen were the popular lekking places of the blackcocks. This morning there were no birds on the grass hillocks, although it was as yet early in the day. When I first knew Rothiemurchus there was no little lochan by the Iron Gate. This pond, for it is little more, has come into existence within the past half-century. I remember the first time I saw a pair of mergansers on this lochan, and the birds nested there that year. Nearly every year now sand-pipers nest on its fringes. Some years, as in 1967 and 1969, the water dwindles appreciably, but since it came into existence I have never known it to completely dry out. The lochan by the Iron Gate still seems to be a popular rendezvous for some of the travelling birds; a sort of temporary watering-place, perhaps. This spring I was rewarded with the sight of a pair of migrating greenshanks.

The Iron Gate is always padlocked, so as to prevent cars from penetrating farther up into Glen Einich. This is a good thing as a file of cars up this rough road could cause chaos; certainly the intrusion of such mechanical contrivances, with their noise and clamour, would be highly undesirable in this lovely, pristine place. The track itself is also hardly safe for the average car, and landslides are not infrequent where the road emerges into the more open country below the long ridge of the Sgoran Dubh Mhor. The first part of the road, once past the gate, runs through a section of the original Caledonian Forest. At Windy Corner—there is a Midgy Corner as well where, sheltered from the winds, the biting species of *Culciodes impunctatus* can be a terrible torment on a warm summer's day—the glen begins to open up until the Loch of Einich itself comes into view. There are no trees here, only long slopes of heather which give way to moss and scree towards the summit of the surrounding hills.

Just before coming to Midgy Corner, Mattie suddenly disappeared amongst the dense bracken beside the path. She came out of the undergrowth quickly back on to the track with a red roedeer doe behind her. The roe was using her forelegs like a pair of flails, and every time she came for the terrier she grunted like a rootling hog. She was a gallant mother, for I have no doubt her behaviour was due to the fact that she had a kid, or kids, concealed somewhere amongst the bracken. This was just how the roedeer doe would tackle a marauding fox should one chance upon her young offspring.

A little way past Midgy Corner I once witnessed a pitiful tragedy. A sparrow hawk had plucked a young fledgling pipit from its nest, somewhere in the heather, and was perched on the decayed stump of an old Scots fir stripping his catch, whilst all the while the parent pipit flew around the static hawk uttering piteous cries. Glen Einich has also been the scene of human tragedies. Once when two young lovers tried to climb the treacherous face below the Sgoran they fell to their deaths. Murdo McKenzie, the second stalker at Glenmore, eventually spotted them through his telescope when searching for them, three days after they had disappeared. On another occasion a retired army officer was lost in the woodlands for three days; he was found nearer dead than alive. Murdo once more was his saviour. The colonel's springer spaniel was seen near his body, and it was the warmth of the dog, who had lain beside the man, that had kept him alive.

Once clear of the woods it is a good walk along the glen past the two derelict bothies beside the path to Loch Einich. Both these stone dwellings are now only heaps of rubble. In the past they were once inhabited, and then subsequently used as temporary stabling for the stalker's deer ponies. Their dereliction, and eventual utter ruin, have come about slowly—stone by stone, as it were. Wind, wild weather and man have all, in part, contributed to the destruction of these ancient shielings. Now on the grass swards beside the tumbled granite boulders, which once made up the walls, campers sometimes pitch their highly-coloured tents and unfortunately leave their tins and paper behind.

Some people consider Loch Einich a long, dark, dour water, whilst others, in contrast, believe it to be amongst the finest lochs in Scotland. Because of its remoteness and situation there is something romantic about Einich, and like many another mountain loch it can change its mood very quickly. One moment it can be bright and sparkling in the sunlight, and then in another second it can become black with great menace. I ate my packed lunch by the remains of the second bothy within sight of Einich's shores.

On the way back I climbed a little way towards the ridge of the Sgoran, and then by the loch of the Long Thin Man, from whose waters, in the days gone by, I had taken many a small trout. Then, instead of dropping down to the track, I struck into the fringe of the old forest of Rothiemurchus, above Loch an Eilean. This ancient woodland is always an exciting place because, if you move silently, both the pretty little crested tit and certainly a great cock caper, as large as a turkey gobbler, will show themselves.

Red deer, roedeer and red squirrels are some of the wood's permanent residents. There is a herd of red deer hinds in these woods. The members of this cervine community are essentially woodland animals, and as such are closer in affinity to the original red deer of Britain which were almost entirely forest-dwellers. These deer live in the woods in summer and winter, for the woods are cool in summer with their shady, umbrella-shaped fir trees, and warm in the snows of winter with their abundant, long, rank heather and juniper scrub amongst which the deer find shelter.

It is rough going in this part of the forest of Rothiemurchus, but there are many paths made not by man but by the red deer who dwelt here long before man came. Whenever I find myself within the premises of this old wood of Caledon I expect to see primitive man appear, clad certainly in skins, with his sling or bow and arrows, hunting for his meat, for Rothiemurchus is a changless place.

CHAPTER IV

A Land of Memorials

Between the banks of the river Spey and the foothills of the Cairn Gorm hills people have erected, at various times, a surprising number of rather unusual mementoes to men and women of no particular renown, but all of whom have had one great thing in common—a deep and everlasting love of the countryside where their names still remain engraved in stone. In the minds of many of us memorial stones, plinths and monoliths are more likely to be associated with graveyards than the open moor and the forest; but here on the fringe of the Cairn Gorm hills are a number of memorials, every one of which has been placed in a site of considerable natural beauty. One could easily spend a month's holiday simply discovering these rather unusual contributions to the memory of some man or woman now departed from this life. It would be perhaps an unusual quest, but certainly not necessarily a morbid one.

There is a cairn on the summit of Kennepole Hill above the lovely little Highland loch of Gamhna, which was erected to a Duchess of Bedford, who was a daughter of Lady Jane Maxwell, then the Duchess of Gordon. The Duchess of Bedford, who was closely associated with the neighbouring property of Kinrara, was evidently in the habit of taking a somewhat lengthy stroll from the tiny loch of Gamhna to the top of steep Kennepole Hill where there is a curious recess in the rocks, once believed to be the den of a wild cat; so that even now this well-wooded hillock is sometimes referred to as the Hill of the Wild Cat's Cairn. The view from the summit of Kennepole towards the Sgoran and the wild Corrie Buidh is one of surpassing beauty. The monument on top, for it is far larger than the average hill cairn, is interesting; its inscription is typical of many others to be found on these local memorials.

The engraved tablet of grey Aberdeen granite says:

To her whose eye explored
And whose step marked
With discriminating taste
This little path
From Loch Gamhna to the
Cat's den and round
the Craig of Kinnepole
to its Summit
This simple tablet is inscribed
by a sincere and affectionate friend

On the reverse side of the memorial another plaque has been inserted. This one is of pink Peterhead granite and reads:

Johannes Bedfordiae Dux
Posuit

Overlooking the loch adjacent to Gamhna—the famed Loch an Eilean—there is a massive, solid block of stone with an inscription on it to a gentleman who lost his life in the loch owing to a skating accident. This monolith was erected by the people of Rothiemurchus in memory of Major-General Walter Brook Rice, of the Royal Artillery, who was accidentally drowned whilst skating near the spot.

There is a cart track which runs from the north end of Loch an Eilean round Achnacoichen to the modern iron foot-bridge which crosses the Beinne towards the well-trodden pass of the Lairig Ghru. Within sight of this bridge there is a tall stone boulder, again of Aberdeen granite, which was placed there by the friends of one Helen Campbell Hughes. This is an attractive monument, and it somehow conveys, in a re-markably potent manner, the love that Helen must have felt for the grand country in which the memorial to her now stands. She did not die in the hills or in the Lairig Pass, the way to which her commemoration stone now guards, she was the victim of a German flying bomb which killed her in London on June 30th, 1944. One feels, after reading the inscription on this rock, that during the period of this lady's life in bomb-torn London, during the war, that there surely must have been many occasions when she would have thought of, and longed to be amongst, the everlasting peace and quietness of the high hills of the Cairn Gorm range.

If you come back to Coylum Bridge from the Hughes memorial by the Iron Gate to Loch Einich and Whitewell, on the left of the path, out on the bare moorland, stands a rough cairn of piled stones surmounted by a large single boulder on to which has been affixed the bronze insignia of the Glasgow University Officers Training Corps. The remains of Hugh Alexander Barrie, M.A., are stated to be interred within the pile, whilst those of Thomas Baird, M.A., whom this cairn also commemorates, are said to have been interred at Balder-nock. These two men were the casualties of a climbing accident in the nearby hills.

Tragedies still occur. Organisations such as the Mountain Rescue Service, which consists of a splendid body of volunteers from the district, all of whom have an intimate knowledge of the Cairn Gorm and Monadhliath ranges, and the R.A.F. rescue team, have done much to save lives; but there are occasions when the over-adventurous, and more probably the irresponsible, get lost, find themselves snow-bound or injure themselves, and then death overtakes them. Scarcely a year now passes without such casualties. I have myself taken part in searches after lost persons, and inevitably one feels very deeply the sadness of these tragic endings. The words on the Barrie-Baird cairn read simply:

Find me a windswept boulder for a bier

This is remarkably apt, and somehow strongly conveys the sentient thoughts of those adventurous spirits who in their life-times have accepted and gloried in the challenge of the hills.

A Land of Memorials

Within a mile or so of the camping site in front of Glenmore Lodge, in the adjoining Forest of Abernethy, there is a nicely worked granite monolith. This stone has been sited so that from its base one can see the Pass of Revoan and the mighty mountain of Cairn Gorm itself. This is a monument erected to James Hamilton Maxwell who, so says the inscription, loved these hills and who was killed in action in the trenches near Ypres in 1915 at the early age of twenty-two.

These are but a few of the many memorials which one is apt to come across in one's travels through this region. The valley of Spey has proved, through the ages, to be a kind of repository of commemorative monuments from tall columns dominating some hill, such as the memorial at Kinrara, to the plain boulder of rock by the Lairig path.

CHAPTER V

The Rusted Shoe

The wide Corrie Buidh (Buidh is the Gaelic for yellow), within sight of Loch an Eilean, is a wild, primitive place. Its lower slopes, down to the level of the loch, contain a part of the old woods of Rothiemurchus. There is much dense juniper, long, rank heather and many big, red, original Scots pines. The paths of red deer, and roedeer, wander here and there; most of them eventually to disappear as though the animals themselves, tired of using them, had taken to the dense vegetation. It can be both exhausting and exasperating to start off into this jungle by following a well-worn deer path and then discover that it suddenly comes to an end.

One day I decided to enter this forest with the object of climbing through it to the ridge of the Sgoran from where I expected to be able to look down into Loch Einich. The midday July sun shone in a sky of deep, cloudless blue. A soft wind from the south-east did little to cool the air. I had taken off my jacket and was carrying it over my arm. The soft yellow moss, up above the tree line, was criss-crossed by the tracks of the red deer. Many of the deer that warm day would have abandoned the heat of the corrie for the high tops above.

Approaching the belt where the pines become scattered and the long rank heather takes over, the stick I was carrying suddenly struck metal. The clink of its brass ferrule on some iron object stopped me. Amongst the churned-up, mica-flecked peat I discovered a small crescent of iron heavily encrusted in rust. The thing looked more like a large magnet than the usual horseshoe; it was narrower in the waist and less circular than the modern steel pieces with which our horses and ponies are shod nowadays. I wondered whether the shoe had been cast by some old deer-stalker's garron or had been dropped by some ill-shod trekker's pony, but the shape and the obvious age of the metal piece completely contradicted either possibility. It was cooler up here, and the silence was almost oppressive.

Looking down towards Loch an Eilean, between the old conifers, a shimmering haze of heat lay over the track running from Loch an Eilean to the Iron Gate, by Achnachoichen. Somehow the scene below reminded me of one of those old faded yellow prints which show explorers, in sun helmets, trying to hack their way through vast, impenetrable jungles. The sudden crack of a dried twig, when I stepped on it, alerted two roedeer who sprang from their couch amongst the rank heather to go bounding off out of my sight amongst the clumps of cranberry bushes. I found a comfortable seat, at the foot of an ancient gnarled Scots pine, one of the last on the slope above the thick woodland. A pair of crested tits teetered in the branches above. I put down my coat and stick and began to examine the iron shoe more carefully. The rust had caked hard and it was not easy to flake a part of it from the metal beneath. I remembered seeing somewhat similar shoes in southern Ireland and in the Balearic Islands, where the working mules and donkeys are usually shod.

It was whilst I was handling and wondering about the history of my iron shoe that I thought I heard the distant murmur of many faraway voices. The low hum of sound resembled the singing of myriads of insects. In a clearing amongst the trees below I saw the movement of some living creature.

The men sat in small, select circles, each group around a little smoking fire. I saw that they were all deeply tanned. Sikhs from the Punjab, with their bearded faces and tall turbans on their heads sat apart. Dogras from Kashmir and Pathans from the north-west frontiers of India were in separate groups. All the men were dressed alike in khaki uniforms. Beyond the squatting men, ropes had been tied from tree to tree, and tethered to the lines by rope halters, at regular intervals, were scores of mules. Their pack saddles and mountain-gun equipment had been neatly placed on the ground in long straight lines, in front of the mules' heads. A tall man with a pale complexion was walking among the animals as if he were inspecting them. By the appearance of the badges on his tunic he looked like some sort of officer. The scene was fantastically clear out there in the brilliant light of the summer day.

During the 1939–45 war, when I was stationed in London as a desk-tied warrior in the R.A.F., I would occasionally escape, on my leaves, to Strathspey and particularly Aviemore and Rothiemurchus. This part of the country had not escaped the traces of war, for it had been selected as the training ground for troops from as far afield as Norway and India. Glenmore Lodge and Forest Lodge were largely Scandinavian centres. Aviemore and Rothiemurchus both had their quota of men from the armies of India. Most of these men, if not already mountain men, were being initiated into the art of mountain warfare in anticipation, it was said, of the invasion of Norway.

On one of my leaves I had come upon the carcase of a splendid horse in this very corrie of the Buidh where I was now sitting. It had been a lovely, fine-limbed chestnut mare, obviously some officer's charger which had had to be shot, out there on the hill, because of some accident.

I noticed that the group of Pathans below me were eating a sort of flat, brittle bannock, which one of them broke off from a large, round loaf. The men muttered whilst they ate. A tall, turbaned Sikh rose from his squatting to walk over to a restive mule which was pulling at its tether on one of the lines. I cannot remember now how long I sat there beneath that old, gnarled Scots pine, but the scene below changed very quickly, for the sun became suddenly obliterated by a patch of black cloud and I heard the quick rush of wind in the pine needles above my head. The crested tits were silenced, but the soft murmur of men's voices continued, and the occasional snort and stamp of some impatient animal.

A dun-coloured red deer hind stepped out from behind a big clump of juniper, and then another and yet another. The hinds,

The adult peewit with proud, upstanding, feathered crest

The cairn on Cairn Gorm's summit

Derelict bothy on the Pass of Revoan

with a number of calves at foot, fed peacefully in the clearing below. I rose from my seat, which immediately brought the hinds to gaze. With one long look they vanished into the thick tangle of the primeval wood of Rothiemurchus. There was no longer any sign of mules or men.

When I got back to my car, which I had left by Loch an Eilean's shore, I found that I was still carrying the rusted mule's shoe in my hand. In some strange manner, I am now convinced, that old piece of rusted metal had acted like a sort of Aladdin's lamp carrying me back, over the span of years, to the time when soldiers from all over the world were massed in the Scottish Highlands to do their training in order to rid the world of the Nazi menace.

I still have that shoe, for it now lies with my other precious, valueless trophies on the window-sill of my study. When I got home I showed it to our farrier, who is a skilled equine pedicure with several letters after his name. He examined my find carefully and diagnosed it as a donkey's shoe. When I asked him could it have belonged to a mule, he said, "Yes, why not?"

CHAPTER VI

Seeking Shelter from a Storm

The early morning weather forecast had predicted "showers with sunny intervals". One of the sunny intervals was on when I walked, through the lovely Pass of Revoan, along the track which leads from Glenmore Lodge to the old Forest of Abernethy. This is truly beautiful country on the northern fringe of the Glenmore National Park. Emerging from the wooded ravine on to the open moorland beyond, a cloud came over to obscure the brilliant sun. The landscape darkened as the first shower swept over the moors. When I entered the grove of old Scots pines, which is the beginning of the Forest of Abernethy, the sun was shining once more.

A big cock capercaillie slid off a tall pine tree, above the red-brown path now damp with rain. The silence of the great bird's take-off was somehow surprising. A little farther along the track a roedeer doe, in full red summer coat, barked—somewhere close her kid was likely to be crouching. Coming out of the trees a small herd of red deer hinds and calves crossed the path.

Passing by the little reed-fringed lochan by Rynettin, the blackheaded gulls rose and screamed. The first drops of rain speckled the water as another shower approached. Towards the west a great bank of black cloud began to build up. Poised above the square green fields of the croft, two small stone buildings, with red-rusted iron roofs, suggested possible shelter from the approaching storm.

By the time I reached the croft the rain was coming down in sheets. The windows of both the stone dwellings had been knocked out, and there was no sign of humans anywhere. Out on the grass sward, about the two cottages, a few black-faced sheep with their milk-white lambs grazed. A stocky dark brown gelding stood in the shelter of a cottage wall. The pony would be used for carrying deer when the stalking season was on. Seeking shelter from the rainstorm, I turned the brass knob of the front door of the smaller of the two stone dwellings. The weather-washed, green painted door opened easily on its creaking hinges. Inside the place smelt of damp and dry rot. The rain drummed on the metal roof, creating an all-pervading vibration. The place looked as if a herd of bullocks had trampled through the house. Above the mantelpiece a mezzo-tint of Windsor Castle hung awry upon the wall, its glass shattered into a hundred pieces.

A yellow grained-oak chest of drawers stood drunkenly in one corner on three legs; on it was a mahogany mirror-stand minus the glass. Old leather harness hung in shreds on the walls. A disembowelled deer saddle had spewed its stuffing over the floor. In one corner of the room there was a pile of assorted spring traps. Examining them, I found one which seemed big enough to take a bear. The fox and rabbit traps were badly rusted and quite useless.

In a number of wooden boxes there was an extraordinary assortment of odds and ends. A scarlet and orange cardboard packet contained great brass rifle cartridges of ancient loading. A 16-bore pin-fire shotgun cartridge was still heavy with its original charge. A hammer gun, minus its stock, leaned in one corner of the room. Porcelain and odd crockery, all broken in some place or other, filled two cartons. A pair of carriage candle lamps, both showing rust in patches, had been stacked beside the iron grate of the open fireplace.

The floor, whose bare boards were still mostly dry and bearing, was littered with modern magazines now mass produced for the teenage group. One lurid cover showed a young man in blue jeans sprawling over a golden-headed girl amidst a sea of green and yellow daffodils. *Secrets* was the title of the paper. The room lightened suddenly when the storm swept over. The dust raised by my intrusion glittered in the sunlight now streaming in through the vandal-smashed windows. Looking out towards the south above the Pass of Revoan, I could see the high ridge of Mam Suim. I was examining one of the old brass outsize cartridge cases from the orange-coloured packet.

It was on Mam Suim's shoulder, many years ago, that I had first met the occupant of this Highland shieling, Peter Hamilton, who was then the stalker at Forest Lodge. I had gone out with Murdo McKenzie, our second stalker at Glenmore, to the march above the Green Lochan. Deer had been hard to find until late in the afternoon we came upon a lone stag close to our boundary with Forest Lodge. Hoping that the beast might decide to come our way we decided to approach him. It had been an even chance that he would wander away from us into our neighbour's ground. When we had got ourselves within rifle shot he was over the march. I looked at Murdo, and I am sure the nefarious thought that was in my mind to poach the stag must have translated itself to him, for he looked at me and winked. I slithered over the peat to get into a good position for the shot. Suddenly the stag sprang forward with a convulsive leap to crumple in a heap. The sound of the rifle shot followed almost at once.

We lay still for a while until the neighbouring stalking party showed themselves, then we went forward to meet them. The sportsman who had shot the stag had with him the professional stalker from the croft, a very tall man with particularly penetrating eyes. Murdo and he spoke to one another whilst I congratulated the man with the rifle on his excellent shooting. Chance meetings like this on the hill happen more often than is generally realised. The image of that professional stalker in his rough tweeds and fore-and-aft hat and his staff and old leather-cased telescope, was a picture which somehow made a deep impression on my mind.

The storm had now nearly passed, and the rain had lessened with the coming of the sun. Looking through the paneless window I heard the snort of a horse, and then I saw riding along the forest path across the close-cropped turf of the croft an old man with grey hair, riding a dark brown gelding. He wore a fore-and-aft deerstalker hat and an old tweed coat, and his plus-four trousers had been stuffed into a pair of long rubber boots. Across his shoulder hung an old telescope encased in a dark brown leather case. The rider went out of my sight down the path towards Forest Lodge. The sun was shining again as I emerged from my shelter to take the rough track to Nethybridge. The dark brown gelding still stood with his broad rump up against the stone wall of the bothy. Water dripped from his mane as he dozed in the welcome warmth of the bright sunlight.

That evening, after I had returned to Nethybridge, where I was staying, I went along to see my great friend William Marshall of Coire Cas. I mentioned, in the course of conversation, that I had been that day through the Pass of Revoan and had sheltered from a rain storm in the Croft. I had said nothing of my vision when William Marshall remarked:

"Peter died this past winter."

CHAPTER VII

William Marshall—Naturalist

William Marshall of Nethybridge on the little river Nethy, was the head forester of the extensive Seafield properties which extend into Inverness-shire, Moray and Banff. As a planter of trees few men were his equal; his knowledge of all botanical matters was comprehensive. But it was Marshall's wide experience of the wild birds and animals of his native Scotland, and particularly of the Strath of Spey, which immediately impressed anyone who met him.

Born in 1884 in western Argyll he had come as a boy to Inverness-shire where he lived nearly all his life. He was over eighty years of age when he died in 1968. After a long day in the Seafield forests he would spend his evenings observing the lives of the wild birds and animals. Starting work in the forests, he had quickly realised that he had a natural interest in all the living and growing things around him. This curiosity towards natural history was an inherited characteristic, for both his father and his grandfather were naturalists of some local repute.

After leaving school at thirteen, young Marshall had spent most of his weekends during the summer and winter watching birds and animals. In the summer he did it the hard way, sleeping out in the open. On weekends, as he always had to be back at work early on Monday morning, he used to make long forced marches into the more inaccessible hill districts. There were few places in the Cairn Gorms, or the Monadhliath mountains, which were unknown to him.

When he was young, Marshall was more interested in wild animals, but as he grew older birds began to claim his attention; eventually he became conversant with the ways and habits of nearly all the species, although he was the first to admit that the older one got the more one realised how little one knew of any particular creature. Marshall's knowledge of the ecology of our two native deer, the red and the roe, was comprehensive. The notes he had compiled on the habits of the red grouse, black grouse, capercaille and ptarmigan could have filled several books.

He used to write pungently with a particular flavour all his own. For years he had contributed a column to the *Northern Scot*, and at one period he wrote a fascinating monthly series for *The Gamekeeper and Countryside*. These precise, accurate pen portraits of Scottish wild-life would have made an interesting volume if they had been collected and published as an anthology. It was rather characteristic of Marshall that he seldom wrote under his own name, preferring a pseudonym, so that his provincial writings usually appeared under the pen-name of Mam Suim, whilst his articles in *The Gamekeeper* all appeared above the words Coire Cas, the name of his house where he lived in Nethybridge.

Nearly all of Marshall's short holidays were spent in furthering his knowledge of natural history. In 1948 he went to Iceland to study the nesting of the pink-foot goose. In 1947 he spent three weeks in Caithness trying to locate the nesting sites of the greylag and the common scoter. He was particularly concerned to learn whether these two species could still be classed as British mainland breeders. The results of his searches revealed that the common scoter had established breeding colonies in Caithness. The greylag, when Marshall made his investigations, appeared to have forsaken the mainland—all he discovered was a brood of greylag goslings which had been hatched off by a domestic hen; the eggs had been picked up from a deserted nest out on the moors. One year he went to Stockholm in order to watch the Manx shearwaters. He then went to Dorset and Hampshire to see the Dartford warbler. One summer holiday he spent in Ireland where he found that Irish whiskey, after his own native dew of the Spey, tasted like varnish!

Many famous naturalists and ornithologists used to call on him to consult him on various problems concerning the birds and animals of the British Isles, amongst them people with international reputations like Frances Pitt, Seton Gordon, James Fisher, the Reverend F. C. R. Jourdain, Professor V. C. Wynne-Edwards and the then Duke of Rutland. There were others as well; it would need a large visitor's book to hold all their names. Scarcely a week passed when someone of renown did not call at Coire Cas. Marshall sometimes referred to the famous as "the big boys", but when he said this he meant no malice. He would chuckle and make some wry comment about the value of radio and television in their dissemination of knowledge about the wild-life of the world and his own immediate countryside.

Like so many great men, Marshall's charm lay in his modesty. His one passion was facts. He might allow himself to conjecture about the ways of the wild, but he also went the limit to prove whether his findings were right or wrong. He was in the tradition of another famous Scottish naturalist, Thomas Edward of Aberdeen, whose life and story Samuel Smiles, the author of the well-known *Self-Help*, immortalised in *The Life of a Scottish Naturalist* published in 1876.

If anyone is entitled to a memorial in the lovely, wide Strath of Spey, that man is surely William Marshall.

Buzzard's nest on Kennepole Hill

The ridge of the Sgoran

Loch Spynie's reed beds contain a wonderful variety of birds

Peter Hamilton was the stalker at Forest Lodge

The beautiful scavengers of Loch an Eilean

Loch an Eilean is certainly amongst Scotland's most lovely lochs

CHAPTER VIII

Loch Spynie

Over a century ago Charles St. John of Elgin in Moray, the well-known naturalist and sportsman, made the Loch of Spynie famous by his writings. In his book *Natural History and Sport in Moray*, he says:

"Loch Spynie I consider to be about the best loch in the North for wild-fowl shooting. Its situation is excellent and, being for the most part shallow and covered with grass, rushes and tall reeds, it is perfectly adapted in every way for sheltering and feeding all sorts of wild fowl and they resort there in incredible numbers and of every kind from the swan to the teal."

Since these words were written, there has been remarkably little change at Spynie. The loch itself is situated close to the harbour of Lossiemouth, and it is almost within sight of the North Sea. To any storm-tossed birds, migrant geese or swans, it must appear as a very welcome placid stretch of calm water when viewed at altitude from out at sea. The loch certainly attracts many migrants, from the smallest of all European birds, . the tiny goldcrest, to the greatest, the mighty whooper swan.

The old ruins of the Castle of Spynie dominate the loch and its surrounding vast reed-beds. This is a relic of considerable interest. The reed-beds and the adjacent marshland contain a wonderful variety of birds, and such rarities as the osprey, as well as unusual visitants to the north of Scotland like the marsh harrier have been recorded.

One day in spring, having first obtained permission from the owner of Loch Spynie, Captain James Brander Dunbar of Pitgaveny, I visited this famous stretch of inland water. I made my way through the fir woods, by Scarff Banks, to find the Loch of Spynie as I have always known the place, unchanged and as attractive as when St. John wrote of it. There were not many birds afloat as it was the time of their nesting, and most of them were concealed amongst the surrounding reed-beds and marshlands. The fringes of the loch were vibrant with the song of the lesser birds.

Walking along the side of the loch, northwards in the direction of Lossiemouth, I was entering a strip of old conifers when I heard above my head a considerable commotion. A great bird burst out of the top of a fir tree carrying in one foot a trout of about half a pound in weight. The osprey flew skywards, then circled around the south shore to disappear from sight above the Castle of Spynie, still carrying the fish. Convinced that there was a nest about I began to look for it. There was little time, as I had an appointment in Elgin at two o'clock. I scanned the tall fir trees in the immediate vicinity of the loch with my binoculars, but without success.

Later I heard a rumour that a pair of ospreys had built a nest within half a mile of where I had seen my osprey that day with a fish in its talons by the Loch of Spynie. The actual site of this nest was said to be in the old wood of ancient Scots pines between the Spynie canal and Arthur's Bridge.

In the past the old wood was a favoured haunt of a number of fine roebucks and it was also the site of an extensive heronry. In those days there must have been thirty or forty nests in this heronry, but now the number is far fewer. In recent years the neighbourhood of this lovely old wood has been much disturbed by gravel extraction, and there is constant aerial activity —and the ear-shattering noise of numerous screaming aircraft. Some herons still persist in nesting in this ancient site, and it was in this colony of herons that a pair of ospreys had tried to bring off a clutch. Whether or not they succeeded has not been confirmed.

Ospreys abroad, in the eastern states of North America and in parts of Scandinavia, are themselves colonial nesters. It would appear to be a clever move for a pair of British ospreys to pick a site like this one, amongst a colony of herons. For with the constant coming and going of the herons the ospreys would be far less noticeable than if they were to choose a solitary site on some tall fir, such as they have done elsewhere at Glenmore, Insh and Loch Garten.

The trout-fishing in Loch Spynie is certainly amongst the best to be had in Scotland. Spynie is shallow, and its waters have access to the North Sea through a series of man-made canals which enter the river Lossie less than a mile from the loch itself. One of the reasons why Spynie's fishing is of such quality is, undoubtedly, because it is regularly stocked with fresh fish. This is done with fingerling trout taken from the estuary of the Lossie. Netting the river mouth for these little fish is carried out, at set intervals, during the spring months of the year. As the river here is tidal the water has a high degree of salinity. A purse net is used with which to take the trout, and the time selected is when the tide is at its lowest ebb; this enables the net handlers to wade the river in thigh-length boots during dragging operations.

The bag end of the net is expanded with fir branches so as to prevent its mouth from closing, and a number of round stones are then inserted in order to keep the net close down on the river's sandy bottom. Two men are able to operate the trawl. The first takes one end and then wades across the stream until he reaches the far bank, whilst his assistant pays out the net. When the net is stretched across the river the trawl begins and a long sweep is made towards a convenient stretch of sand on to which the purse-net can be hauled.

Salmon and sea trout are occasionally taken, but the bulk of the catch usually consists of flounders, river trout and such odds and ends as minnows. Large portable metal containers stand ready on Lossie's banks, filled with the brackish water taken from the estuary. The skipping brown trout are picked off the beached net and immediately placed in the metal containers. When a sufficiency of fish has been netted the carrying cans are quickly conveyed to the Loch of Spynie in a van. This whole operation usually takes under an hour; there is virtually no mortality amongst the fishes during the actual process of the netting, for the trout are transferred whilst the dabs, flounders, eels and other oddments are all thrown back into the river.

It seemed strange to me, at first, that these fish caught in highly saline water should survive so well once they were introduced to the fresher water of Loch Spynie. It is well known that salmon, sea trout and eels migrate from fresh water to the sea and vice versa. The stickleback can survive equally well in fresh or salt water. The dab or flounder, a marine species, will travel long distances up-river to places where there is scarcely any trace of salinity. Both brown, or yellow, trout and rainbows, taken from lakes or rivers, well away from the sea, will often thrive in salt water.

A recent report from the Danish marine biological institute records that perch, pike and roach—all regarded here as essentially freshwater fishes—have been caught in the sea around the coasts of Denmark. The famous *truite bleu* of the Continent, so greatly relished by the gourmet, is often Danish brown trout fattened in sea water and then conveyed in special containers to France, Belgium, Holland and Switzerland.

This adaptability on the part of certain fishes is well illustrated by the successful, regular Lossie–Loch Spynie transfers, and the subsequent excellent sport these very lively fish provide for those so fortunate as to be granted a day's fishing on this lovely Loch of Spynie.

CHAPTER IX

The Ospreys of Strathspey

Few birds can have had more ink expended upon them than the much-publicised ospreys of Strathspey. A record of the ospreys' return to Scotland as a breeding species has been published by The Royal Society for the Protection of Birds. This brochure is by George Waterston, R.S.P.B., who has been largely responsible for the ground organisation of watchers and custodians during the birds' nidification periods. There is also an excellent foreword to this work by W. J. Eggeling, B.Sc., Ph.D., F.R.S.E. Conservation Officer, Scotland, The Nature Conservancy. In this booklet is contained most of the data any layman needs who is interested in *Pandion haliaetus*.

I was watching a pair of roedeer amongst the marshes on the fringe of Loch Mallachie, which has an outlet into Loch Garten, when I saw my first Scottish osprey. At the time I was engaged in making observations on the roe of the district. The fact that I was festooned with a pair of powerful binoculars may have given me the appearance of a bird-watcher or even egg-collector. Anyway the bird appeared not far above my head, flying along the southern extremity of Loch Garten. As it was unusual I put my glasses on it. It was impossible to say whether the fish-eagle was a cock or a hen.

I was quite fascinated, and entirely absorbed in watching the bird, when an authoritative and very indignant voice requested me to absent myself at once. I did not go, for surely I had as much right to be where I was as had the owner of the commanding voice. I stayed, to be invited into the hide from which the ospreys were then being observed; and it was here that I became witness of a most extraordinary incident.

Mrs. Waterston, once she realised that I was only an enthusiastic amateur roe-specialist, was exceedingly kind. Looking back on this episode I can well understand her agitation, for almost at the very moment when I appeared on the scene an attempt was being made by some vandal to rob the nest under observation of its eggs. It was a remarkable coincidence, and at the time George Waterston and two of his male assistants had just departed at high speed in a car to try and circumvent the egg-robber. The thief had put the hen bird off the nest, and as I could see for myself with my binoculars, she was reluctant to settle down again.

Whilst we were watching, a pair of hoodie crows came into view. Crows are as bad as human oologists when it comes to egg-lifts, and it was obvious that these carrion birds had their eyes on the osprey's nest and its contents. Fortunately, at this very moment George Waterston and his assistants arrived at the hide from their unsuccessful attempt to apprehend the human stealer. Seeing the hoodies George Waterston immediately instructed his helpers to blow their whistles. Three police whistles now sent their strident screechings across the marsh-lands. The noise appeared to have the desired effect, for the crows speedily departed from the scene.

Eventually the ospreys resumed their nesting, but tragedy came shortly afterwards, as during the hours of darkness the egg-thief came back to make a most horrible mess of his thieving; for he must have dropped the eggs which were found broken beneath the nest. There are no words sufficiently strong with which to condemn this act of utter vandalism; an act which far surpasses any of the marauding adventures of the men of old like St. John, John Colquhoun and Lewis Dunbar, be-cause today we ought to have advanced a little in our attitude to wild-life and the conservation of rare species such as the osprey.

In 1959 I was at Nethybridge when the ospreys arrived. This time they chose a new nesting site not far from the old one. I have often wondered whether the memory of the pre-vious season's tragedy influenced these birds to seek a fresh situation in which to prepare their nesting arrangements.

The bird protectionists were now much better organised, and out in force. Largely due to their vigilance the ospreys nested and successfully brought off their clutch. Three young were reared. This attempt, on the part of the ospreys, to re-establish themselves in our hostile land, was now national news. The press, the B.B.C, the other television authorities were all in on it. Like the Derby, the Grand National, the Queen's Birthday and Christmas Day, the annual visit of these fish-hawks became a seasonal event of considerable interest. Every year thousands of people in cars, on bicycles, in buses and on foot began to arrive at Loch Garten to see the ospreys.

The re-establishment of the osprey as a breeding species in Britain has been well recorded by Phillip Brown and George Waterston in their book *The Return of the Osprey*. This was no easy return, for time and time again the birds were frustrated, and usually the human offenders were vandals or egg-collectors, and not the much vilified keeper and sportsman.

In 1963 I was staying once more at Nethybridge when the nest used by the ospreys was blown out by a gale. One year the tree in which the birds were nesting was nearly sawn through by senseless barbarians. The damage was discovered in time and the tree and the nest on top saved by strapping the tall conifer with iron strips.

After the gale destroyed the nest, the ospreys sought fresh quarters elsewhere; on one occasion I was able to watch a remarkable display of nest-building on the part of the displaced birds on a lone, bare pine tree near the Ranch. An osprey would take off, at regular intervals, from the partially constructed eyrie, to make a circle in the woods where there were a number of dead Scots pines. As the bird passed a dead tree it would snatch a limb in its claws, break it without pausing in flight, and then carry the piece to the nest where the hen was waiting ready to receive the timber for her new home. Very rarely did the cock bird drop a stick, and usually these were brought safely to the site where the hen was perched. Some of the branches were formidable pieces, requiring a good wrench to break them off the parent tree. Although I was able to watch this second attempt at nesting more than once, the ospreys never seemed to settle, and they eventually appeared to lose interest in this so-called "frustration" eyrie.

In 1963 a pair of ospreys came to Insh, and almost within sight of the loch itself attempted to complete a fresh nest, but to the best of my knowledge no young have ever been reared at this site. I kept a score, for seven years, of the Garten ospreys' breeding attempts:

1958   The Year of the Vandals. No hatch.
1959   3 young reared
1960   2 young reared
1961   3 young reared
1962   1 young reared
1963   No young reared
1964   3 young reared

Through absence in the spring of '65 and '66 I missed the ospreys. The year 1967 saw three chicks successfully reared. Since the mid-sixties ospreys have increased in this part of Scotland, and there are a number of regular nesting sites. One, in particular, is within sight of a big car-parking lot on the broad highway from Glenmore to Coylum; but few people seem to know of this nest's existence. Birds certainly nested there in 1968 and 1969.

In the spring of 1966 a snowy owl was observed near Glenmore. Hamish Marshall, a nephew of William, saw this bird at close quarters. Hamish is nearly as good a naturalist as his late uncle. He is a member of the Mountain Rescue team and spends as much time as his work with the River Authority permits in and about the Cairn Gorms and the Monadhliath ranges. Snowy owls have been reported as nesting in this range of mountains before, but there appear to be no accepted records of any of them rearing young. The snowy that Hamish Marshall recently saw was a single bird, and so far as is known, no mate ever appeared on the scene.

The calves of the red deer are born in May and June

Most deer, by their nature, are forest-loving animals

Highland red deer are a diminutive variety of the red deer race

In 1967, however, a pair of snowy owls nested in the island of Fetlar in the Shetland group. They successfully reared six chicks out of a clutch of seven eggs. One proved addled. This ornithological incident hit the headlines of the lay press. The radio joined in. Television was quick on the scene. It was all a splendid piece of publicity work on the part of the R.S.P.B. It was decided to put these birds up to public view like the ospreys. Wardens were brought into action. An observation hut was erected. The owls proved superb hams. They were so much more photogenic than the rather disappointing ospreys of Garten.

The Times produced a spread of photographs of the owls of Fetlar. *Country Life*, for September 21st, 1967, showed a lovely shot of the female snowy owl in threat display. Few other birds when photographed show more human features. Somehow, nearly every adult snowy owl looks like a furious Colonel Blimp with bristling grey moustaches and glaring eyes!

W. Kenneth Richmond, who wrote the article on the snowy owls of Fetlar which accompanied the photograph in *Country Life*, mentioned that during his visit to observe these birds he and the warden were interrupted by a lone human who loomed out of the mist, causing dismay to the female owl who was then still attendant on her six chicks. The human intruder was immediately approached by the writer and the warden. The man explained that he was a botanist searching for a rare chickweed, and he had become lost in the fog. He was warned off without more ado. Reading this fascinating account of the snowy owls of Fetlar brought to my mind my own experience by Loch Garten when I stumbled upon the ospreys' guardians when quite innocently trying to observe some roedeer!

Snowy owls are big birds, though not quite the largest of the owl family, as the European eagle owl is bigger still. Romantic wild-life writers have referred to this bird in phrases such as: "The great, silent, ghost-like killer of the vast arctic wastelands."

Snowy owls are efficient avian predators living, in their

normal arctic habitat, on various hares, lemmings and other species of the tundra lands. They have erupted from the arctic circle on numerous occasions, and have wandered far south. One was found in Bermuda.

It is conceivable that a pair of snowys may one day decide to favour some out-bye part of the Cairn Gorm range or the Monadhliath mountains as a nesting site. Such an event would most certainly provide a gala day for the press as well as the ornithological circles, but whether it could provide an avian exhibition on the lines of the Loch Garten osprey's annual show would largely depend upon the accessibility of the site chosen, as well as its defensive possibilities—for there are still avid egg-collectors and vandals in our midst.

A long way from Spey, but well worth a visit, are the snowy owls now to be seen in a nearly full feral state in Norfolk. These are the magnificent owls belonging to Philip Wayre of the Wildlife Park near Norwich in Norfolk. They are lovely birds and appear completely content in their present extensive quarters.

CHAPTER X

The Beautiful Scavengers of Loch an Eilean

The beautiful scavengers of Loch an Eilean are its black-headed gulls. Loch an Eilean is certainly amongst Scotland's most lovely lochs. Situated in the old forest of Rothiemurchus it is surrounded by birch thickets and ancient Scots pine trees. There is a track which runs around the loch, and from it may be seen a splendid variety of wild birds and beasts. This route has now been made into an admirable Nature Trail, a guide to which may be obtained in the shed at the north end of the loch. Produced by the Nature Conservancy, and illustrated with delightful pen and ink sketches of local fauna and flora, it is a most useful little guide to the locality and remarkably cheap at a few pence.

Such varieties as red deer, roedeer, woodcock, buzzard, crossbill, crested tit, goldcrest, goosander, mallard, wigeon, goldeneye, merganser, heron and, of course, the blackheaded gulls may appear. In the spring and summer the gulls which frequent Loch an Eilean seem to be almost as numerous as the chaffinches, perhaps the commonest bird in the vicinity.

The gulls of Loch an Eilean are almost entirely confined to the species *Larus ridibundus*, an inland nester; although black-headed gulls do not appear to nest about this loch itself they certainly do so in considerable numbers in many stretches of water in the immediate neighbourhood. Seagulls today in many parts of Britain have become almost an inland race. This is not really surprising, for Britain is a small island not difficult of access in all its parts to strong-winged birds like gulls.

The greatest scavengers amongst the gull family appear to be the blackheaded gull and the herring gull; and although these two species are often seen together, the former appears to be more of a land scavenger, whilst the latter likes the seashore, river mouths and particularly harbours where refuse is generally abundant. Herring gulls must consume a prodigious amount of offal cast overboard by ships of all sorts. Fishing trawlers coming home to port, with the gutting of their catch in process, are sometimes enveloped in a cloud of scavenging gulls.

All the gulls are lovely birds to look at, although it must be admitted that some of them appear to have the most disgusting habits. The two kinds of blackbacked gulls, for example, are credited with a revolting kind of cannibalism, as during the nesting period a blackback will sometimes snatch the hatched young of another pair and devour them. Both the greater and the lesser blackbacked gulls are serious menaces to sheep farmers and the game rearer. A pair on a moor may well prove more destructive to both the eggs and chicks of grouse than a number of hooded crows, and they often kill lambs.

The greater and the lesser blackbacked gulls should not be confused with the blackheaded gulls, and they are easily distinguished, for even the smaller of the two blackbacked gulls is far bigger than a blackheaded gull being, in fact, nearly the size of a herring gull, whilst the greater blackback is larger still. In appearance, too, they are quite different, their most pronounced likeness perhaps being in the names that man has given them. The blackheaded gull, particularly during the breeding period, is a very lovely creature with his dark brown cap, which looks at a distance like a close-fitting black hood, and his crimson beak and legs set off with the pure cleanliness of his light plumage.

The blackheaded gulls of Loch an Eilean are a somewhat sophisticated community, and the sight of a stationary human being, or particularly a motor car, on the shores of the loch, will immediately bring an inquisitive bird to its vicinity. In a remarkably short space of time another will follow, and should there be any picnic scraps about the air will very quickly be full of scavengers. Unfortunately, these refuse disposers of Loch an Eilean do not seem to be able to digest such items as wrapping paper, cigarette cartons or cellophane. The latter surely is the most persistent of all forms of rubbish as it seems to be well-nigh indestructible.

In all fairness to Loch an Eilean's many visitors today, on the whole they are remarkably litter-conscious; although there is not a single litter bin or receptacle to be seen around its lovely shores, there is very little refuse. All and every form of edible reject is quickly attended to by the beautiful unpaid bird scavengers of the neighbourhood, and unedible material is presumably buried or taken home by the human visitors. This is certainly a most admirable state of affairs, and one on which the many sightseers to Loch an Eilean may well be congratulated.

The so-called common gull, which is rather surprisingly not all that common, is seldom seen at Loch an Eilean, although this bird is no great rarity in the district. The common gull, or mew gull as it is sometimes called, is about the same size as the blackheaded gull, but it is not such a striking character, being less brilliant in appearance, and I am rather inclined to think less vocal in the air. The common gull's light grey plumage and pale yellow legs make it look rather like a mature herring gull, but considerably smaller. Common gulls usually nest in the far north of Britain and for this reason, if for none other, they may well be claimed to be a very Scottish bird.

All the better-known gulls such as those mentioned in this chapter have the habit of following the plough. A tractor churning the earth nearly always has its attendant flock of gulls, whether it be ploughing a smallholding far up in the hills or in the wide Strath of Spey.

The family *Laridae* consists of many species and some of them, although they have been recorded in Britain, are very rare. The little gull, Audouin's gull, the slender-billed gull, the glaucous gull, the Iceland gull, as well as certain others, come into this category. However, the greatest rarity of them all is

Ross's rosy gull, an arctic species, of which only two instances have ever been recorded in this country. Such sea birds as the fulmar, kittiwake and tern, although they all look rather like gulls, are not really gulls at all.

CHAPTER XI

Birds of the Grouse Family

Lagopus scoticus, the red grouse, named for Scotland, is a valuable economic asset to this country. In certain lights these birds of the moorlands are golden-brown in appearance. They certainly bring much welcome gold to Scotland from England over the border, as well as from many other foreign countries.

Americans, in particular, are very fond of *Lagopus scoticus*, and they pay considerable amounts to the inhabitants of Scotland for the privilege of shooting these birds. The red grouse, in the opinion of many experts, can provide the finest form of flying shooting. One reason why Americans like to come to Scotland to shoot grouse is because at home they are strictly limited by legislation as to the amount of game they are entitled to kill in a day or a season. The American sportsman, no matter how wealthy he may be, will sometimes go out and shoot four cartridges at pheasants, or such birds as the remarkably named Timber-doodle-dandies (woodcock), and he will have then reached his legal limit. Here in Scotland he may shoot several hundred cartridges in half a day, for provided the birds are there, there is seldom any reason to pause.

It is not unusual to have to pay as much as £500 per week per person for the privilege of pursuing *Lagopus scoticus*. A recent report in *The Field*, giving the grouse-bags achieved in various parts of Scotland, listed the names of some of the guns participating in a day on an Inverness-shire moor. There were no less than three princes, two counts, one baron and two plain monsieurs! Between them they bagged 786 grouse in four days' shooting on this moor. Moreover, the number slain was not by any means exceptional.

The red grouse is a problem bird. A great deal of literature exists concerning its life and habits, and yet we know very little about it. Much money has been spent, in the past, on research concerning its ecology, and this still goes on. It is a mystery to many of us why certain parts of Scotland are favoured by this game bird whilst others have lost the greater part of their stock.

There are a number of good moors in the Strath of Spey, but some places where good bags were once obtained, have depreciated considerably. Not so very long ago red grouse were plentiful in Glen Einich and Glenmore; now they are scarce. The constant intrusion of numerous humans has had an influence. Lack of keepers and increase of vermin is another cause, but there are other factors as well. Some parts of the west of Scotland, where grouse were once plentiful, hold few birds today. The climate of the west has been blamed, but this surely is not the sole reason for the paucity of grouse.

The grouse unit of Aberdeen University, amongst other bodies, continues to investigate the life of this bird so that one day we may eventually know more about *Lagopus scoticus* than we do now. Fortunately there is at present little likelihood that the red grouse will become extinct as did its far larger relative the so-called giant grouse of Scotland, the capercaillie.

The caper, *Tetrao urogallus*, became extinct in Scotland towards the end of the eighteenth century; some authorities have suggested the year 1769, but there are others who have maintained that this great bird of the grouse family lived on, in pockets, in western Inverness-shire and Glenmoriston until 1815. The reason usually given for the caper's decline was the decimation of Scotland's forest, the chieftain grouse being a bird of the woods. The name capercaillie is derived from the Gaelic *cabhar-coille*, which means a bird of the woodlands.

It seems entirely improbable that *all* our moorlands will be planted or ploughed up, so that a change of terrain is unlikely to eliminate *Lagopus scoticus*; but where afforestation takes place, and this is happening widely in Scotland today, the red grouse nearly always eventually disappears.

The disappearance of the capercaillie from the Scottish scene caused concern to a number of people, and in 1837 a successful scheme to reintroduce the caper was undertaken by a combination of philanthropic individuals. Lord Breadalbane, the owner of considerable properties in Scotland, after consultations with Sir Thomas Fowell Buxton, purchased a number of adult capercailles in Sweden, and then had them brought over to Scotland. This purchase was arranged through a Mr. Lewellin Lloyd, a Swede with a very Welsh name. Lawrence Banville, an experienced gamekeeper, was chosen to go over the North Sea to collect the birds. Fifty-four adult capers of different sexes were successfully shipped to Scotland in a schooner chartered for the job.

The birds were eventually released—presumably as pen-reared pheasants are now—in the wooded districts of the upper Tay valley. Subsequently there were several introductions on a lesser scale, and also a number of spasmodic attempts to place caper eggs in greyhens' nests, so that today *Tetrao urogallus* is once more a well-established bird in Strathspey and other parts of the Scottish mainland.

The brevity of the extinction period, if we can take 1815 as the final year of the capercaillie's elimination from the Scottish scene, is very short—only twenty-two years in fact. I must confess that on more than one occasion in the primeval pine forests of Rothiemurchus and Abernethy, where capers are quite abundant today, I have allowed myself to wonder whether some birds, at least, were able to survive in the depth of these great, dense woodlands so that the blood of our native stock has never ceased entirely to flow.

One day, very early in the morning, I was driving from Nethybridge to Loch Garten through the pine woods. In a clearing within sight of the unmetalled road a cock caper strutted and clicked. Against the russet background of a bracken-clad mound he looked enormous. The pale sunlight, shining on his plumage of purple and turquoise green, made the bird a glorious sight. His great wings trailed, rustling the stalks of the dead bracken. His tail was fanned like that of a peacock in display. His neck was stretched out, whilst he kept calling *pick up, pick up, pick up* with ever increasing rapidity. Suddenly his love serenade ended with a sudden *plop*, just as if a champagne cork had been neatly withdrawn from its bottle. Somewhere amongst the bracken a hen must have been crouching, but I never saw her. Capercaillies are generally silent birds, both in their flight and in their song—if you can call it song.

The most vociferous of the grouse family is undoubtedly the blackcock; he is, in fact, a regular Caruso. Blackgrouse are becoming scarcer nearly everywhere. Not long ago they were numerous in parts of the Spey valley, and it was no unusual thing to see dozens of these birds together in Glenmore and parts of the Forest of Rothiemurchus. Now you may see a few if you are lucky. The blackgrouse of these districts cannot have disappeared because of changed terrain, for the country hereabouts has not materially altered. In other places where blackgrouse were once plentiful the situation is different, for the kind of country this bird prefers has been encroached upon.

The blackgrouse is a bird of marginal land lying between the heather and old mature timber, places where silver birch flourishes and bracken grows. On close-cropped grass fields by the fringe of the woods these beany blue-black birds have their lekking places. This sort of country is today being increasingly planted with trees, and if the soil is not too shallow it is being reclaimed for agricultural usage. Hence the land loved of the blackgrouse is gradually becoming increasingly scarce.

On the green mounds by Whitewell and Tullochgru, within a few minutes' walk from Coylum Bridge, blackcocks used to gather to sing their love-song in the dawn. The chorus of these birds is extremely penetrating, and the sound carries for considerable distances. It is a melody hard to describe, for melody it is. A sort of *rok, kok, kok, kok-rok, kok, kok*, on and on, with a timeless lilt about it which ululates far over hill and dale. Blackcocks certainly do not confine their singing to their mating amphitheatres. I have watched a sole cock, perched on a stone wall, with his scarlet eyebrows aflame and his neck stretched out, singing lustily in evident ecstasy. Sometimes, and particularly when on the lek, the chorus of a congregation may be interrupted by one individual sneezing. This sound is an abrupt *tish-shoo*, but almost at once the song will be taken up again by the others present in a series of *rok kok rok koks* containing a rhythmic ebb and flow which in some peculiar manner results in a melodious harmony. Strangely, the female, or greyhen, seldom if ever participates in these sonatas.

The British grouse bird least affected by mankind is undoubtedly the ptarmigan or mountain grouse. Almost entirely confined to altitudes above the 1,500-foot mark, these delightful game birds are free from man's farming or forestry activities. There are no chemical sprays or soil disturbances in their natural habitats, so that only severe weather or undue wet can harm them, and the ptarmigan is an extremely tough bird. It has to be able to survive in the cold, bleak conditions so often prevalent at high altitudes. Some of the finest ground for these grouse of the high regions exists in the great ranges of the Monadhliath and the Grampians.

One day, whilst walking the ridge above Corrie Beinne which looks down on to the long glen of Einich, I heard a queer sound. It came above the crunch of my steel-studded boots on the wet, glistening granite chips. It was a grinding, gritting noise, just as if two pieces of quartz had been quickly rubbed together. *Kee-ack* and then dead silence, then the voice came back again from somewhere amongst a pile of tumbled rocks. The scuttling shape of the grey-white ptarmigan was almost reptilian as the bird ran over the moss-covered stones uttering its strange alarm call. The ptarmigan is perhaps the least vociferous of all the British grouse family, for apart from the grating noise it sometimes utters, it hardly calls at all.

The red grouse, although not particularly loquacious, has quite a wide vocabulary, and in many ways the sounds made by these birds are more like those of barnyard fowls than are the voices of any of his other relatives. Red grouse will cluck and chortle to one another, but their most persistent refrain is a quick *go-back, go-back, go-back,* accelerated to *back back back* at the too close approach of man or dog. Occasionally, when unalarmed and conversing with one another, grouse make a continuous gobbling call which sounds like *kowk-och-och-och-och, ad infinitum.* A study of the language of our grouse birds can be an entirely absorbing occupation.

CHAPTER XII

Golden Eagles

The golden eagle in Scotland is a rare bird no more. Within the limits of the wide Spey valley and the neighbouring Monadhliath mountains and the Cairn Gorm range of hills, there is now a near static resident population. Because the eagle is of such interest to the bird-watcher and naturalist, not to mention the photographer, there are quite a number of people who know where these birds have their territories and are likely to nest.

The Nature Conservancy wardens at Kinakyle and Achnachoichen are certainly amongst those who will have this information, but it is unlikely that either of these men would be likely to disclose it; and unless there was a specific scientific reason for obtaining the whereabouts of the breeding sites of these great raptors it would be unfair to try and probe them. Besides these representatives of the Conservancy there are several others who undoubtedly have the knowledge, amongst them a number of professional stalkers and keepers, and certainly, when he was alive, William Marshall of Coire Cas. His nephew Hamish Marshall, with his experience in the Mountain Rescue Unit, must also be pretty well aware where most of the eagles of Speyside and its adjacent hills have their eyries.

I confess that I love the sight of an eagle. There is something exciting and majestic about the view of this great, soaring bird in the orbit of one's binoculars. But there I am prepared to let it lie. I have no desire to peer into an eagle's nest, or to examine, at close hand, the rather repulsive little downy bundles of pink flesh which are the unfledged eaglets. Their gaping beaks and staring reptilian eyes have, for me, little allure. All my experience of eagle's eggs and eagle's young has been through the cinema, television and close-up photographs. Although inexperienced in the practice of bird-nest photography, I have seen some of these practitioners at work.

Eagles are believed to be multi-nesters, and they frequently have two or three alternative eyries which they will use in different years. Many of these breeding sites have been built over the years by the birds in fairly close proximity. One site is behind the ridge of Mam Suim. There are others below the Sgoran in Glen Einich and opposite the Lurcher across the Lairig Ghru, and still another eagle area in a deep dour glen where the three counties of Aberdeenshire, Banffshire and Inverness-shire meet.

One day I decided to explore the country to the north-east of Glenmore where the ridge of Mam Suim stands out in all its glorious magnificence. This is eagle territory, and Hamish Marshall had told me just where to use my glasses to find a nest. This proved not difficult, and by climbing a quarter of a mile up the opposite face to Mam Suim I was able to get a good view of the eyrie. There was no bird on it, but beside the nest I saw a long, tendril-like object hanging downwards. It was a rope, and beside the eyrie itself someone had built a crude hide.

A quarter of an hour later an eagle came in view. She was a lovely sight as she circled and hung in the air above her nest. Eventually satisfied, she swooped as if to land on the nest. Within five feet of her objective the hen eagle swerved in mid-air, climbed swiftly and disappeared. Ten minutes later a figure emerged from the hide to descend to the bottom of the glen with the aid of the rope. He then climbed up towards where I sat beside a boulder in the long rank heather and proceeded to abuse me for my presence on the scene. It was my fault, he said, that he had missed a chance to get this golden eagle on her nest!

In the Highlands eagles have provided me with a number of exciting episodes. The Mam Suim incident was not one of them. It was decidedly unpleasant. One day when in the birch woods beside Loch Ericht, which is within a few miles of the upper reaches of the Spey, I was to witness a marvellous display by a hunting eagle. It was October and the grey geese were flying southwards down from the far arctic wastelands where most of them breed. A skein of greylags came down the length of the loch at an approximate altitude of 800 feet. Above them a solitary eagle appeared a mere speck in the sky. Suddenly the eagle swooped, his objective the leading goose in the V-shaped flight formation. When the eagle was almost on its victim the flight leader began evasive action and broke from the skein. The bird second in line took over the leadership, whilst the eagle and its quarry went downwards towards Loch Ericht. Having shaken off its pursuer the goose climbed to join its companions once more. The eagle proceeded to gain altitude again to make a second attempt on the formation of geese. He now struck for the new leader, who easily avoided him. By this time the greylags were well down the loch towards Cambusericht and the eagle appeared to lose interest.

Last spring, when in the Nature Reserve by Loch an Eilean, I was lying in the heather with my Jack Russell terrier beside me, when a golden eagle came low over the Inshriach march at an altitude of some 500 feet. The bird never saw me, but noticed the dog. Whether she thought the terrier was a lamb or not is just conjecture. The eagle came down to within ten feet of the ground, questing all the time. She never attempted an attack, but kept on circling like some great buzzard. I have never been closer to a wild golden eagle before. Finally, her curiosity seemingly satisfied, the great bird climbed to make for the hills above Glen Feshie where I knew of the existence of another eyrie.

At a distance buzzards are sometimes easily mistaken for eagles, but the buzzard is much smaller, although its aerial manoeuvres on occasion are very similar to those of the larger bird. The Reverend F. O. Morris, the entrancing ornithological divine and author of a *History of British Birds*, has rightly said that the golden eagle is more like a vulture in its habits than a falcon.

A golden eagle, as a hunter, cannot compare with a swift

killer like a peregrine, a merlin or a sparrow hawk. Eagles kill and eat plenty of blue hares and grouse; they also consume quantities of offal in the form of dead sheep, deer and the plentiful grallochs of the red stags and hinds during the stalking season. Most live quarry is pounced on when stationary, a couchant hare or a squatting grouse. They are indeed grand birds in the sky, but not swift, silent killers like so many of the *falconidae*. A golden eagle on the ground, busy with a dead carcase, will waddle and jump and trail its wings, for all the world like some great vulture of the African plains.

A hummel is a red deer stag carrying no antlers

A red grouse, *Lagopus scoticus*, named for Scotland

I came across
the carcase
of a hind

Foxes
thrive in
the Highlands

CHAPTER XIII

The Red Deer of Strathspey

The red deer of the Scottish Highlands, is, in company with the little roedeer, a true native of this country; and it is certain that both these lovely wild creatures lived in the forests, corries and glens of Scotland long before man ever came to dwell here.

The other British deer, and there are five other species, namely the fallow, sika, Chinese water-deer, muntjac and reindeer, are of foreign extraction, for they have all been brought here at various times by the hand of man.

Most deer, by their nature, are forest-loving animals. From Spain to Russia, and again in New Zealand and South America, where red deer have been introduced, these animals are nearly always to be found in woodlands. Other overseas deer, like the white-tailed deer of eastern America, the sambhur of India, the maral of Iran and the wapiti of Canada, also prefer trees to the open.

Here in Scotland, however, owing to circumstances over which the deer themselves have had no control, they have been forced to take up a mountainous existence in treeless places. Where woodlands exist red deer tend to drift towards them, and it is when the deer infiltrate into the planted forest areas of the Spey valley that they have to be severely dealt with in order to preserve the trees.

Because of its enforced highland existence the Scottish red deer, with the specific name of *Cervus elaphus scoticus*, is now an unusual form of deer in that it is smaller, in stature and in weight, than its immediate relatives the red deer of the European continent, Caucasia and Carpathia. Highland red deer are, in fact, a diminutive variety of the red deer race.

Male red deer carry antlers, the females or hinds are hornless. Every year the stags cast their horns to grow a new set in the spring. For the greater part of the year the males keep together, in bachelor herds; and the females do the same, although the latter may be accompanied by male calves and young stags known as knobbers.

The rut of the red deer takes place in the autumn when the stag herds break up and the individuals set out in search of the hind gatherings.

As in the case of most ungulates it is the coming into season of the hinds which controls the time of the deer's mating. When the rut is on the stags become most vociferous, and then Speyside and the glens and corries of the surrounding hills echo with the awesome sound of the roaring males. The voice of a lovesick stag is a thrilling sound, and it has a considerable range, from a nasal *yick, yick, yick, yick* to a deep booming bellow.

The calves of the red deer are usually born in May and June; and they grow very quickly so that by the time of the adults' mating in September and October, the young are well able to care for themselves. When the rut is past the males and females incline to separate once more, to go their own ways until another season.

In the past the head of a good stag was regarded as a fine ornament, or trophy, by the sportsman. Scottish stags rarely carry more than twelve points on their antlers. A twelve-pointer, if there are "cups" of three points on each horn, is known as a Royal, and is a greatly-coveted trophy.

In order to improve the quality of our Scottish red deer heads much foreign blood has been introduced at times into the Highland deer forests. Great park-fed stags, from such English estates as Warnham and Woburn, were brought to Scotland and released amongst the native stock. In many instances this infusion of fresh blood undoubtedly "improved" the species.

When I was in Braemar recently I saw a very nice thirteen-pointer. The taxidermist who showed me this head felt sure that it was the descendant of a big Warnham stag which had once been introduced to Aberdeenshire with the object of bettering the local strain. The practice of bringing fresh blood into the Scottish Highlands has largely died out since the 1939–45 war; and traces of alien blood, which was quite pronounced in some parts of Scotland during the earlier part of the present century, are now rapidly dying out and the red deer are decidedly reverting to type.

With all these artificial efforts to improve the trophy-value of our native stags, none of them has ever been able to grow the monstrous horns of some overseas red deer. Stags' antlers from countries such as Hungary, Spain, Czechoslovakia and the Caucasus, are simply enormous when compared with the antlers of our home-bred deer. Whereas a Scottish stag seldom goes over twelve points, some of these foreigners not infrequently exceed twenty points.

Although a number of these Continental, woodland-dwelling beasts are huge animals, both in body and horn, I have never seen more massive heads than some I once examined at the International Big Game Exhibition at Düsseldorf in Germany in 1954. These trophies had come from South America, where Scottish red deer were once imported during the early part of the present century. These monster stags, which had benefited in horn and body from the lush feeding of their new home, had grown heads of over thirty points!

Rather surprisingly, the greatest publicists of the wild red deer of Scotland have not been Scotsmen themselves. A certain William Scrope, who was an English sportsman, wrote in 1840 one of the most popular books ever published on the subject of red deer. It is called *The Art of Deer Stalking*, and it went into three editions at least; some indication of its wide appeal. A little later Sir Edwin Landseer, R.A., the great animal artist, painted many pictures of Scottish red deer in their natural habitat.

One of the most famous of these oil paintings is *The Monarch of the Glen*, which shows a monstrous stag against a background of the Cairn Gorm mountains. Reproductions of this picture have gone all over the world, and the original may be seen in Dewar's head office in London.

One Scotsman, however, who made a most excellent study of the life and habits of our wild red deer in their natural surroundings, was Allan Gordon Cameron. In his book *The Wild Red Deer of Scotland*, he has left us a painstaking and detailed study of *Cervus elaphus scoticus*.

The stalking of red deer in the Scottish Highlands is a fairly new form of field sport when compared, for example, with the hunting of deer or the pursuit of a fox or hare with the assistance of hounds. Before the firearm was ever used against deer such weapons as bows and arrows and the arquebus were frequently employed. It was the invention of the accurate sporting gun or rifle which made possible the sport of stalking as it is conducted today.

Before red deer stalking started in the Highlands, deer were not considered a particularly sporting quarry. They were, in fact, merely meat on the hoof to be rounded up and slaughtered whenever flesh was required. The killing of the deer was usually left to the lowlier members of the clans to perform. The customary method of killing the red deer of the hills was to try to herd them towards ambushed men armed with anything which could lay low a deer. Hounds were also sometimes used to course the deer until they became exhausted, when they could be more easily dispatched.

The coming of sheep to the Highlands of Scotland, towards the end of the eighteenth century, resulted in the clearing of much territory of deer. The red deer were driven, by the sheepmen, to the high places where the deer succeeded not only in surviving but also in establishing themselves successfully in such mountainous regions as the Cairn Gorm and Monadhliath ranges.

It was not until the beginning of the last century that deer-stalking, as a form of field sport, began to be properly appreciated; this state of affairs was assisted because the rifle had by then become a sufficiently accurate weapon with which to kill an animal as large as a red deer effectively and efficiently.

Deer-stalking as it is carried out in Scotland today is, therefore, not much more than a hundred and fifty years old—a trifle, in time, when compared with the age of such sports as beagling and buck-hunting with the aid of hounds, or angling with the help of a rod, line and hook.

In spite of its comparative newness there is something essentially ageless about deer-stalking which may possibly be accounted for by the territory in which it takes place; and the methods employed which, in essence, have not changed at all since man first took up a firearm with which to slay a deer. Through all the many changes that have come about in our ways of life since man first began to stalk the deer with a firearm in the Scottish Highlands, the actual pursuit of the stag has not changed at all. The spy to discover one's quarry; the careful approach; the thrilling, perhaps uncomfortable last crawl and the final shot, remain as exciting today as ever.

Stalking as it is conducted in Scotland is almost certainly the most humane of all the field sports. The greater number of deer are killed outright, whilst others are missed entirely. Some, unfortunately, are wounded; but as it is the stalker's unbreakable creed to do everything in his power to get a wounded beast, few escape to linger, and those that do so often recover, as nature is a wonderful healer.

CHAPTER XIV

Stags without Horns

The deer were lying on the slope of Cadha Mor almost within sight of the old pine woods to the west of the track which leads from Coylum Bridge to Loch Einich. They seemed to be enjoying the mid-day warmth of the late September day. Watching the animals through field-glasses I saw a hind rise from her couch among the heather, her calf of the year following her example. Soon all the deer were on foot. There were six hinds and three calves. The deer seemed suddenly restive.

The hummel came down wind from the direction of the pine woods, his great bull neck stretched out like a hunting hound. He was making towards the hinds in a hurry. Through the binoculars his mouth appeared to open, and then, seconds later, his lovelorn roar came ululating over the high moorland. The voice of the stag was like the distant lowing of cattle, but with a menace in it. The bald-pated red deer stag was a gross brute, obviously heavily larded, as the expression is. He was a powerful animal; he looked rather like a light, lithe bull, but no member of the *bovidae* could have displayed the grace of that hummel out there on Cadha Mor.

A hummel is a red deer stag carrying no antlers. They are rare; just how rare nobody really knows, although some experts have attempted to estimate their numbers. These estimates vary from one in a hundred normal stags to one in five hundred. Hummels are interesting animals. Normally a hummel stag will outweigh an antlered male of the same age.

His head, bare of antlers, has two slight knobs, not much bigger than a couple of fifty-pence pieces in diameter. These protrusions are completely covered in hair without any trace of coronets which would indicate, at least, an attempt at horn growth if nothing else. The pedicles on the head of a hummel look rather like the bumps one sees on the head of some polled breeds of cattle, like the Red Poll and the Aberdeen Angus. One big difference between deer and cattle is that stags grow a fresh set of antlers every year, whereas horned cattle grow their horns once and for ever.

This annual horn growth on the part of male deer—for the females of red deer, like the rare hummels, carry no antlers— is a draining process. Stags, who come to rut in September and October, and are run down as a result of their exertions, cast their antlers early in the following year when feed on the hills is at its poorest. Now the antlered stags have got to build up their bodies and, at the same time, provide their frames with enough nourishment in order to produce a new set of antlers. The hummels, having no horns, do not have to contend with this dual seasonal drain on their systems. Consequently they are generally bigger and heavier animals than their normal brethren and because of this, when the rutting season is on, in late autumn, they are often successful in winning the hinds for themselves.

One might well imagine that any animal with antlers could beat one without, in a fight, but this is not the case, which makes one doubt the effectiveness of antlers as offensive weapons. The hinds themselves appear to be unselective of their male companions, and a hummel would appear to be as welcome to them as an antlered monarch; but then hinds are notoriously promiscuous in their choice of mates, as they will normally accept the first and then the strongest that comes along; and this is where the hummel wins.

It is almost a universal belief in the deer forests of Scotland that a hummel, if he does not actually beget a hummel, at least, does not breed good heads; in the past, as fine-antlered stags were desirable in a forest, most stalkers had it in for the hummel. There is no doubt about the potency of a hummel stag—one has only to watch one with a herd of hinds during the mating season—but whether the hummel is fertile is a matter which is still in some doubt.

Reliable observers have suggested that the presence of a hummel in a particular district nearly always results in a deterioration of the horn growth of a number of the male deer of the neighbourhood. Some years ago a hummel stag was observed in the island deer forest of Jura. A few years later the general horn growth of the Jura stags was said to have declined, the inference being that the hummel was responsible for this deterioration.

My own observations of hummels has led me to believe that they vary appreciably in numbers at different periods. They seemed to be much more numerous ten or twenty years ago than they are today. At one time, when a hummel was shot, the fact usually received a certain amount of publicity, but this does not seem to happen now.

Some years ago I saw in Glen Einich no less than three hummel stags in one day, but during the past ten years I cannot recall having seen a single hummel. Of course, this does not necessarily mean that hummels have declined in number during the past decade. The old credo that a hummel breeds a hummel may have contributed towards a slight decrease in numbers. There is also the fact that an abnormal creature has an appeal for certain types of sportsmen, and so the known presence of a hummel in a deer forest becomes a powerful incentive to lay him low. In both these respects the hummel would appear to be proscribed, either because of the suspicion of his bad breeding taint, or because his abnormality makes him a desirable trophy.

Nowadays, when in most deer forests the quality of venison is so important and heads, certainly, less of a status-symbol, one would imagine that the fatter, heavier, hummel would be a desired resident in a forest! They are strange-looking animals these antlerless male deer—odd in more ways than one.

Ord Ban's cairn is a simple pile painted with Snowcem

The great stag's hoof marks in the peaty soil looked like a bullock's

The name capercaillie is derived from the Gaelic.

The Grampian mountains have always been a stronghold of the wild cat

In Rothiemurchus roedeer have existed since time immemorial

CHAPTER XV

The Herd of Ord Ban

Sir Frank Fraser Darling, ecologist, biologist, conservationist and prolific writer, had published in 1937 a book entitled *A Herd of Red Deer*. This concerned the study of the red deer of three deer forests in Wester Ross, in the far north of Scotland. Darling was able to undertake this survey as a result of the grant of a Leverhulme Research Fellowship and the ready co-operation of the forests' owners. It is a quite fascinating book, and is certainly one of the best British wild animal records ever written. Darling's study of *Cervus elaphus scoticus*, the Scottish red deer, is wide, comprehensive and meticulous; and it is unlikely to be superseded for a very long time.

It is probable that it was this author's influence which, subconsciously perhaps, caused me to take such an interest in the herd of Ord Ban over a period of twenty-five years since the end of the last war in 1945.

Ord Ban, and its neighbouring conical-shaped mount Kennepole Hill, overlook Loch an Eilean in the Cairn Gorm National Nature Reserve. Both hills have man-made crowns on their summits. Ord Ban's is a simple pile, painted with Snowcem; why the usual cairn of stones has been thus deco-rated, I do not know. Kennepole's crown is more unusual, and not all that easy to find, as Kennepole's peak is largely afforested; here is the monument of granite, inscribed and dedicated to a former Duchess of Bedford, described earlier.

Loch an Eilean and the surrounding land are a part of the Rothiemurchus Estate, owned by Lieut.-Colonel J. P. Grant, of Rothiemurchus. The area to the east, beyond the deer fences, is the covenanted land of the great Cairn Gorm National Nature Reserve. The twin hills of Ord Ban and Kennepole are about 1,400 feet, and lie respectively to the west and south west of Loch an Eilean. Due south of Loch an Eilean is the little loch of Gamnha, or the Loch of the Stirks, for the surrounding land was once used for grazing young cattle. The herd of red deer resident on the eastern shores of Loch an Eilean keep almost entirely to the hill of Ord Ban, and I have never seen them on or around Kennepole, although the distance between the bases of these two conical-shaped hills is at one point less than a quarter of a mile.

The vegetation on Ord Ban is varied, and consists of Scots pine, silver birch, extensive bracken, juniper, broom and, higher up, long, rank heather. The botanists have identified over two hundred species of flowering plants. The western slopes of Ord Ban and Kennepole run down in the form of permanent pastureland to the Inverdruie–Inschriach road which travels parallel to and above the river Spey. Across the Spey is the main A9 road from Perth to Inverness—a highway which has constant traffic on it through night and day. These roads, and the river between them, restrict the red deer of Ord Ban from travelling westwards. To the east of the two hills a deer fence runs due north and south, up to and between the lochs of an Eilean and Gamnha; this fence continues along the Inschriach forestry to Invereshie and Glen Feshie beyond. It is a quite formidable barrier, but certainly to the red deer no impassable one. Sometimes stags from the neighbouring great forests of Inschriach, Glen Einich, Glenmore and Glen Feshie cross into the Ord Ban area by skirting the deer fences where they enter the two lochs of Gamnha and Loch an Eilean; but at other times they somehow get through the wire fence itself.

One day this spring I came upon the carcase of a hind which had got its legs entwined in the wire fence between Gamnha and Loch an Eilean, and had died of starvation. These tragedies are rare, however, because in October when the stags come to the hinds on Ord Ban, they seem to be able to get in and out and to and from the outlying deer forests without any trouble. Deer are known to be excellent aquatics, and the short distances

74

across the two lochs would be no serious deterrents to such good swimmers.

The herd of Ord Ban is essentially a resident, feminine society. Adult stags seem to appear amongst them only in the late autumn, and somehow it always seems that these females come into season rather later than the norm, as the rut about Loch an Eilean always appears to occur *after* the time of the roaring in the adjacent deer lands. It is, in fact, what is called a hind forest.

The first time I came upon the hinds of Ord Ban was in the spring. I was walking around this conical hill about half-way up an altitude of about 700 to 800 feet. Turning into a small corrie overlooking the Spey I saw twelve deer, eleven hinds and yearlings and one knobber who had not yet cast his horns. I am inclined to think that at that time (1946) this may have been the total population. In the autumn of 1969 I counted twenty-two deer, twenty-one calves and hinds and one knobber. The calf crop appeared to have been a good one. Although mid-October, there was still no adult stag with this herd. I was to come across some rather urgent evidence of attempted invasion a little later, for one morning, after crossing the fence at the south end of Loch Gamnha, I walked along the Inschriach march which contains fine forestry plantations. There is a tall, well-maintained deer fence, difficult for man or beast to cross. All along its length from the Invershie march to Loch Gamnha a great stag had ranged up and down. His hoof marks in the soft peaty soil looked almost as large as those of a bullock. The imprints of this male told their own story—a big stag on the rut anxious to get amongst that harem of hinds around Ord Ban. That stags, at this time of year, go through the wire there is no doubt; the annual calf crop of these ladies of Ord Ban proves it. It would also appear that, once satisfied, the visiting monarchs of the adjacent glens go back once more by skirting the fences, or swimming the lochs, to the neighbouring forests.

The deer of Ord Ban do not always keep together in one

herd, sometimes they split into two or more small parties; but more often they are to be met with as a single unit. One day in autumn, before the big stags got to them, I came across six animals lying close together in a bed of bracken on the south side of the hill. Later that morning, on the north-east flank, I found the rest of the herd in a miniature corrie. The knobber, by now quite familiar to me, was with the second party. Incidentally, roedeer are quite common on both Ord Ban and Kennepole hills. There appears to be no antagonism between the two species.

The hinds on Ord Ban have their own wallows. One particularly fine one overlooks the Spey on the east side of the hill. When I last visited it this glutinous black peat mire was a liquid morass with strands of deer hair floating on it. Hinds have their wallows as well as stags, although I have no doubt that the occasional visiting Romeos in the late fall will also make use of their female consort's miring conveniences.

I believe it is usual to take a small annual cull of the deer on Ord Ban, and this would seem entirely necessary for fear of overpopulation. The cull does not appear to unduly disturb the local population, for these deer never seem to want to leave this quite restricted area.

The main thing that impresses one about these deer is their extraordinarily strong territorial sense, and also the fact that they appear to be completely satisfied and healthy in a very limited area. I have never seen the herd on adjacent Kennepole, although the feeding there would appear to be equally as good as that on Ord Ban. The other interesting feature is the fact that this area is yearly becoming more and more attractive to tourists, hikers, bird-watchers and others. The constant presence in the immediate vicinity of crowds of humans does not seem to worry these wild red deer at all, whereas in neighbouring Glenmore, where before the ski-lift came and the human hordes arrived, there were plenty of red deer about, there are now virtually none.

CHAPTER XVI

Foxes of the Highlands

There is a wooden hut, painted forest-green, in a lovely glade in a part of the old original woodland which still exists beyond Loch Gamnha on the Inschriach–Rothiemurchus march. You come upon it suddenly, and unless you know just where it is it is not easy to find. Every year in the spring, when I go to Rothiemurchus, I go to see the hut; it has some strange attraction for me. It belongs to the Forestry Commission trapper, and there are large fox traps as well as rabbit traps neatly stacked in one corner. The hut is never locked, and it has been used on several occasions by hikers and campers from nearby Rothiemurchus and Glenmore. There is a small note inside which says, "Please leave this place as you have found it." There is also an old square biscuit tin on the table, in which grateful shelterers have left notes of thanks and appreciation for the shelter they have obtained. There are candles in the cupboard and a tin containing a little paraffin for those wanting to make a fire for warmth. The fox traps have big steel chains attached to large wooden stakes, because the Highland fox is a strong animal and can pull out of the earth pegs which are not sturdy.

The Scottish edition of the *Daily Express* reported recently that nine thousand foxes are regularly accounted for in Scotland every year. How this total was arrived at was not stated. The *Daily Express*'s figure is likely to be an underestimate rather than an exaggeration. In the one county of Northumberland, in the north of England, there are eleven packs of foxhounds. The total tally of these hunting establishments annually reaches nine hundred to a thousand foxes. Some packs, like the College Valley, which has a part of its country in Scotland, kill an average of over a hundred foxes every year. If in a single county a thousand foxes are killed by hounds alone, and many foxes must succumb by other means, then surely the *Daily Express* has not made an overestimate.

In Scotland the total fox-kill by hounds is infinitesimal for, except on the Borders and in isolated parts of Renfrew and Fife, there is not much mounted fox-hunting. The greater mass of Scotland is not hunted. The majority of the Scottish vulpine race are either trapped, shot, gassed or poisoned. In the hills I have come upon the remains of foxes poisoned and trapped as well as those which have eventually succumbed from gunshot wounds. The gin trap is still a legal instrument in Scotland for the taking of foxes and otters. It is illegal south of the border.

Richard Waddington, in an excellent book on grouse and moor management, has stated that in a period of three years more than two thousand foxes were dealt with in one small corner of Moray and Banff. The Spey separates these two counties for an appreciable part of its length. There is a considerable population of foxes all along the course of the river from source to mouth, and the neighbouring mountain ranges harbour their full quotas. The fox is a night hunter, and unless sprung or disturbed during the daytime, he is usually to be seen engaged on his affairs, either predatory or matrimonial, early in the morning and towards dusk—that is why he is so seldom seen.

Dr. Harrison Matthews, the eminent zoologist, in his book on British mammals, gives a figure of ten thousand foxes killed in a limited area in Wales. There is a considerable similarity between the mountainous regions of the Principality and parts of the Highlands of mid-Scotland. Foxes undoubtedly thrive in both areas. On a grouse moor the fox is very nearly public enemy number one. Any keeper, worth his salt, will undoubtedly make life intolerable to a fox known to be on his beat.

Brian Vesey-FitzGerald has written an excellent book about foxes, *Town Fox, Country Fox*. In this work the author gives as his estimate a figure of forty thousand foxes killed annually in Britain. He shows how this figure is arrived at by quoting a series of local estimates which he considers to be reliable.

One day, out on the hills beyond Kingussie, I was walking through a birch wood to get out on the open moorland above. When about to emerge from the woodland I saw something move out on the hill beyond. It was a small herd of seven red deer hinds. They were bunched close together like a single entity, and were on the move with that long swinging gait so typical of this species of deer.

Behind them, trotting quietly along, was a large red dog fox. He was hunting the line of the deer with his nose to the ground like a retriever after a wounded bird. Suddenly, he stopped to gaze at the deer; the deer also stood to look back at the fox. The fox sat on his haunches to scratch an ear as if he were quite disinterested in the herd above. He turned now to come towards the edge of the silver birch wood where I was standing. Before reaching it, and when he was in a fold of the ground out of sight of the deer, he turned to take a circular route so as to get above the hinds. Having achieved his purpose he now started to run the deer as if he were a collie dog collecting errant sheep.

This game, for there appeared no other explanation for it, went on for nearly a quarter of an hour, and then the fox seemed to have had enough for he set off uphill as if he had never even noticed the deer. The calves in the herd were so well grown that they could scarcely have been distinguished from their dams, and so far as I could see there was no weakly or injured animal in the herd, so the fox could not have been hunting for food. He may just have been stirring up the red deer for fun or devilment. Foxes hotly pursued by hounds have been known to chase and snap at barnyard fowls as if in irritation. They are certainly fascinating animals.

There is still in the Highlands, as well as in other parts of Scotland, a considerable belief that there are two separate breeds of foxes, the hill fox and the lowland fox. The former is nearly always said to be greyer, bigger and longer in the leg than the latter. In fact, there are no two separate breeds. The truth is that foxes vary considerably in size, colour and weight. There are small red foxes in the Highlands, and big grey foxes in the lowlands. Many people still think that every fox has a white tip to his brush, but this is not so.

One reason why the two-species belief has arisen is because, during the past century, and possibly early in this one, a considerable number of foxes were introduced to Britain in the interests of foxhunting. A figure of a thousand foxes imported through Leadenhall market *per annum* has been quoted. Foxes from as far afield as Spain, Austria, Germany, Hungary, France, Russia and Sweden were, at various times, brought to Britain so as to increase local populations. The majority of these imported foxes were of the species known as *Vulpes vulpes crucigera*, but some of those from Sweden were said by the systematists to be a different sub-species, *Vulpes vulpes vulpes*. As the actual difference between the Swedish fox and the mainland European fox is an infinitesimal one of skull size and dentition, the variation, if it exists today, is of little material importance; and certainly the two sub-species, seen side by side in life, could scarcely be distinguished by the professional mammalogist, much less the layman. Dog foxes and vixens vary appreciably in size and weight as well as colour.

Considering the great number of foxes there are in these islands, it is rather surprising how little intensive research has been done on this animal. In so far as Scotland is concerned it is unlikely that any were introduced here from abroad. It is possible that in Scotland's limited fox-hunting areas some fresh blood may have been liberated, but this is more likely to have come from the Highlands and other unhunted parts of the country than from Europe or Scandinavia.

Many Highland keepers and professional stalkers, during the past century and certainly earlier on in this one, did a good business in taking fox cubs from their dens and then selling them for as much as £5 apiece to Masters of Foxhounds in the

Roedeer at times are very vocal animals

The blue hare is in summer a sort of blue-grey dusky-brown

south. This practice has now ceased, and is certainly forbidden by the Master of Foxhounds Association.

Last spring, up a long, winding glen deep in the northern flanks of the Cairn Gorm range—the place shall remain nameless—I came to a stalker's cottage where there were no less than eight dead cubs by his gibbet. In the days of old these cubs alive could have represented as much as £40, at the rate of £5 per head, certainly a worthwhile catch.

CHAPTER XVII

The Wild Cat

It is entirely appropriate that the true wild cat of the Scottish Highlands should be called *Felis silvestris grampia*. The Grampian mountains have always been a stronghold of the wild cat, and at no time in the existence of Scotland has this range of hills been without its cats. The sub-specific name of our wild cat is indicative of this animal's habitat. The description of the Scottish type is to distinguish our cat from the more widely spread *Felis silvestris silvestris* of northern Europe, Spain, Russia and the Carpathians. There are also wild cats in parts of Africa, much of Asia and to the west of China, but these have, like the Grampian cat, been given particular sub-specific names such as *lybica*, *cafra*, *acreata*, *ornata*, etc.

Although I have been so fortunate as to have been able to spend a good deal of time in wild cat country, I have only once caught a glimpse of one when it crossed my path in the Forest of Druimachder which is within the Grampian range. I have often however, come across their tracks, and have been able to examine a number of their kills. Listening to them howling at night can be exciting, and particularly at the time of the rut in March when the toms are after the females. It is scarcely possible to distinguish the screech of a domestic cat from that of a wild one when they are in the neighbourhood together, but when there are known to be no domestic cats in the area and wild cats are about then you can hear the voice of the original. The wild toms scream noisily. The female wild cat is believed to have a gestation period of sixty-three days as against the domestic cat's fifty-eight days. The female is entirely responsible for the rearing of her litter and their education. The male has been known to kill its own kittens.

The Wild Cat

No less an authority than *The Handbook of British Mammals* mentions feral-domestic strains. A domestic tabby which has gone wild on its own account will at times appear remarkably like the true wild cat, and this is well-illustrated in the *Handbook*. The wild cat appears a much more heavily-boned animal than the slimmer domestic cat, and this sturdy appearance is enhanced by the wild cat's broad visage and bushy tail.

The domestic cat's ancestors are mostly foreigners from the Mediterranean countries, but today there are far more of these semi-feral animals about in Scotland than there are true wild ones. These domestic cats which have gone wild are a menace to the countryside as they are highly destructive of the country's natural wild fauna; particularly of its bird-life. Cats as carnivores must kill to live; undoubtedly some of these wandering beasts do good by killing rats, mice, voles and even, on occasion, shrews, but for the purpose of controlling these little rodents there are preferable natural alternatives such as the stoat, the weasel and the owls rather than *Felis maniculata*— the domestic cat gone wild.

The native wild cat of Scotland is an interesting animal, but one which is extremely difficult to observe, and once captured it is well-nigh incapable of domestication. Being almost entirely nocturnal in habit, it is difficult to catch a glimpse of it unless it has been disturbed, or deliberately ejected from its den when the female is tending her kittens. At one period in our recent history the wild cat was thought to be well-nigh extinct, but that some survived successfully there is no doubt, as today these beautiful if ferocious wild animals are now on the increase.

Generally speaking there are two main reasons why a species becomes extinct in a district or a country as a whole. The animal in question may have been of value to man as a fur-bearer and as such a desirable prize, or the creature may have conflicted with man's interests, be they the rearing of domestic stock or the preservation of game for sporting purposes. The bear and the wolf were both eliminated from the British Isles, because they preyed on man's stock. The wild boar, now also extinct, was

a menace to agriculture and sometimes to agriculturists themselves. All three of these animals, however, still linger on in
parts of the continent of Europe because sportsmen like to
preserve a few for their own ends. The beaver was a valuable
fur-bearer and easily trapped so that man killed him for his
pelt. The same thing very nearly happened to the pine marten
here in Scotland, but the importation of foreign skins from
North America and Siberia helped to save him; as well as the
rise of fur-breeding establishments which now produce
millions of skins every year in this country and abroad.

The wild cat's pelage has never been highly regarded by the
furrier, or presumably by the female of the human species as
an adornment for her body. So it was certainly not its skin-
value which was the cause of the near-extinction of this species
during the early part of this century. The real reason was that
the wild cat was an efficient competitor of man in the game they
both sought, which was mainly the red grouse in terrain frequented by the cat.

It was during the heyday of the keeper, in the latter part of the
past century, that *Felis silvestris grampia* was very nearly eradi-
cated from these islands altogether. It was no unusual sight
earlier in this century to see wild cats on Highland keepers'
gibbets. On one occasion I counted no less than four on a gal-
lows by Loch Rannoch. The dwindling of the keeper population, plus the natural reduction of the grouse population in
the far north-western reaches of the Scottish mainland, resulted
in the survival of a remnant of the wild cat tribe in these areas.
Throughout the Highlands today wild cats are far from
scarce.

Wild cats do not make good zoo exhibits because they do not
like to show themselves, and during the daylight hours most
of them try to seek any cover available. To put such creatures
in cages without shade or shelter so that they may be seen is
intolerable. Animals of this kind should not be incarcerated.

The Forestry Commission's policy of continuous planting in
Scotland, as well as large-scale afforestation on many large

private estates, has provided abundant shelter for the wild cat. *Felis silvestris grampia* is a skilful destroyer of mice, voles and other rodents, all enemies of the forester, so that today in many parts of Scotland the wild cat is no longer persecuted.

CHAPTER XVIII

An Abundance of Squirrels

In the summer, when the leaf is on the trees, the early part of the rough track from Coylum Bridge which leads to Glen Einich and the Lairig Ghru is rather like a dark tunnel through the woods. The path comes out into the open where it bifurcates for the Lairig and Glen Einich. It was at this point that I was brought to a standstill one day by the sound of a slight but quite distinct scratching noise. It came from the direction of an old twisted Scots pine, whose gnarled trunk was red as rust.

I looked upwards and there was a red squirrel stretched out along the limb of the tree. We both froze at the sight of each other. The tiny, jet-black, staring, bead-like eyes of the little creature never left my face. In the squirrel's mouth was a fir cone. We stood there looking at each other for what seemed ages. Getting a little tired of this staring match, I turned my head very slowly to look around me.

On the other side of the path there was another old Scots pine in whose higher branches a big domed structure of sticks had been built. The squirrel's drey looked like a sort of hybrid between a crow's nest and a magpie's. I edged backwards inch by inch towards the tree with the drey in it. Immediately the red squirrel on the branch opposite noticed my direction she became violently agitated. Retaining the cone in her mouth she kept on uttering a sort of *tec, tec, tec, tec* deep in her throat. It was evident that the old pine tree held her drey.

Sidling slowly towards the base of the tree I saw a surprising sight; this was a mass of soft blue-black feathers which had obviously come from the breast or throat of a blackcock. The line of the feathers went away from the old Scots pine, towards the dilapidated deer fence which runs beside the Beinne burn.

An Abundance of Squirrels

That there had been a recent murder there seemed little doubt. However, it was improbable that the red squirrel, whose drey was in the tree, was the culprit. Red squirrels will, on occasion, plunder a bird's nest to take its eggs—or the young if already hatched—but a squirrel would be unlikely to tackle an adult blackcock. The scattered feathers were lying along an ill-defined track which looked like the run of a fox. When farther on, beside the fox-run, I came upon fresh droppings, it began to look as if the blackcock's killer was almost certainly a fox.

On returning to the big tree, there was the red squirrel still poised on the same branch. The little creature had evidently no intention of disclosing, by any move on her part, the where-abouts of her home. When I glanced towards her drey once again the squirrel became almost hysterical.

A little way along the well-worn path, in the direction of the iron foot-bridge, there was another squirrel. This one looked quite different from the last. The one thing that both had in common was the light colour of their bushy tails. The second squirrel's body pelage was almost blue-black in colour, whereas the first one's had been bright, rust-red. The second was a melanistic if ever there was one. Nearly every squirrel seen that day showed a marked variation both in the apparent texture of and in the tint of its fur. These animals may have been in a state of moult.

Like a lot of red squirrels, those in Rothiemurchus are re-markably tame. They take little notice of humans except to play a form of hide and seek, by creeping out of sight behind the bole of a tree. There is something extremely attractive about squirrels; in some respects they are almost as cheeky as wild monkeys. A red squirrel will chatter and make faces at a human invader of its territory in a manner which shows quite clearly that it disapproves of man's presence within its own rightful domain.

When squirrels become too numerous in planted woods they can be a serious pest to arboriculture. Their habit of stripping the bark from the upper main stem of certain conifers is particularly destructive to growing trees. In discussing the local red squirrels with the late William Marshall, he told me that in one instance in Abernethy in 1909 squirrels were found to have damaged over 240 acres of Scots pine and larch by ringing the tops of the trees. A single squirrel, he claimed, could damage twelve to fifteen stems in a morning. This destructive habit appeared to be most prevalent in April, and Marshall put it down to a form of cambium-desire on the part of the animal. A bounty of sixpence per tail had to be put on the pests, and as many as thirty were sometimes shot in a day. One squirrel hunter had trained his dog to point squirrels concealed amongst the upper branches of the pine trees.

The females were found by Marshall to have various litter sizes, varying from two to four young, but twins were the more usual. Red squirrels, like quite a number of other British mammals, and field voles in particular, appear to be subject to considerable cyclical fluctuations in their numbers. Seven-year cycles have been mentioned, and it has been suggested—but not as yet entirely proven—that their periods of decline and abundance will coincide with the pine seed fluctuations.

At one period in the past, there is no doubt, red squirrels became extremely rare in parts of Scotland, and it was their seeming absence from the rural scene that brought about a number of reintroductions of these little animals from abroad. Such large landowners as the Duke of Atholl, Lady Lovat and Lady Seafield bought and had released on their properties—which stretched from the Forest of Atholl to Glen Urquhart and across the Spey into Banff—a number of Scandinavian and Continental red squirrels, both of which species are closely akin to our own indigenous Scottish race. That these foreign imports may have interbred with any remnants of the native species is quite possible but, at the same time, quite impossible to prove. The frequent red squirrels one sees at times in the Cairn Gorm Reserve and in other parts of Speyside may be the descendants of imported stock, but it is just as likely, and I believe more probable, that they are of pure Scottish descent.

An Abundance of Squirrels

The importations of these red squirrels, *Sciurus vulgaris*, into Scotland during the past century should not be confused with the more recent attempts to bring the grey squirrel, *Sciurus carolinensis*, to this country. The *Handbook* states that this pest is now to be found in eight Scottish counties, but does not name them. R. S. R. Fitter, however, in his admirable book *The Ark in our Midst*, mentions the importation of a number of grey squirrels at Finnart on the Dunbartonshire shore of Loch Long in 1892. Later, some were released at Edinburgh, whilst a number of releases occurred in 1919 in Fife, the environs of Edinburgh and Ayrshire. By 1944 the original Finnart squirrels had penetrated well into Perthshire, and they may have linked up with the Fife colony.

The grey squirrel has never been recorded in Rothiemurchus, Abernethy or any other part of Speyside. It is to be hoped that they will not immigrate here, for like the emancipated mink, this grey tree-rat from America is an entirely undesirable alien.

CHAPTER XIX

Roedeer

Anyone who is interested in roedeer could not do better than go to Aviemore in order to study these beautiful creatures. Here, within a comparatively limited area, there are many roe and, except for occasional humane control measures, when they are shot with a suitable rifle, they are almost entirely left alone to live their lives in peace, a state of affairs which is the exception rather than the rule in many other parts of Scotland, or at least in the countryside surrounding the Rothiemurchus area. There are certain places in the immediate vicinity of Aviemore to the east of the river Spey where roedeer have existed from time immemorial. Some of these animals have been hunted on occasion in a sporting manner by many a famous roe-stalker since the days of the famous Colonel T. Hawker, who has written with much appreciation in his book *A Sporting Tour through the Northern Parts of England and a Great Part of the Highlands of Scotland* of the attractions of Speyside and the immediate district in and around Aviemore. The Colonel had leave to shoot, fish and stalk here, and he has described his adventures, in this work published in 1804, with a great admiration for the delights and beauty of this countryside.

One suspects that the brothers Sobieski Stuart, alleged descendants of Prince Charles Stuart, must also have at some time followed the roe in the Strath of Spey for, although they have not specifically mentioned Rothiemurchus itself, they have described in considerable detail their pursuit of these animals in the Findhorn valley and on Lagganside. From the brothers' writing in the *Lays of the Deer Forest* (1848) one realises that they placed the roebuck very high in the sporting category; this beast of the chase was usually hunted with the help of a trained hound, or hounds, and finally killed with a rifle, or a gun firing a ball or a suitable heavy charge of shot.

Subsequently, in the latter part of the last century and the early part of this one, there were men such as the professional stalker Grigor Grant, who was born in 1869 in the croft at Revoan—now a tumbled mass of stones much frequented by hikers and campers from Glenmore. Grigor was a famous roe-stalker who studied his quarry, and who seemed to have permission to hunt and stalk wherever he went.

Both John Guille Millais and Frank Wallace followed the roe in Glenmore and Rothiemurchus. These two men, who were great lovers of the deer, have left to posterity some of the loveliest pictures ever painted of our native deer of the hills and the forests. Frank Wallace's picture entitled *Unrequited Affection —Rothiemurchus*, which shows a roebuck chasing his doe beneath the shadows of the Grampians, is certainly one of the finest paintings of these deer in existence. The watercolour shows a roebuck on the rut, the sun is struggling to rise through a clouded sky and, in the distance, a doe stands with her stern to the buck, apparently entirely disinterested in his amorous attention. In this sketch the artist has caught the whole atmosphere of the love-chase, the absolute desire of the male in his search for the female, and the seeming coquettish disinterest of the doe as she feeds quietly on the fringe of a thicket of silver birch. John Guille Millais, who was the son of the famous pre-Raphaelite artist Sir John Everett Millais, has left some delightful studies of roedeer in their different attitudes and aspects illustrated in his various books.

Up until the coming of the Forestry Commission in the Glenmore area, roe were fairly well distributed throughout the wooded parts around Loch Morlich and the Rothie-murchus forest. When tree-planting started around Glenmore Lodge, drastic measures were at once taken to eradicate the roe. Large-scale drives to men armed with shotguns and the use of wire snares were universal. The young trees had to be protected and the deer eliminated. If this object was never actually achieved, the measures taken certainly appreciably diminished the population of roe in this district.

Such destructive tactics, however, were never taken in the neighbouring forest of Rothiemurchus, but a very similar policy of near-extermination was conducted in the forests of Abernethy and the extensive forest plantations around Loch Garten and Nethybridge. In these areas, where some years ago you might have seen a dozen roe in an evening's walk, you will now be lucky to see two. South of Rothiemurchus, towards Inschriach and in the Feshie glen, a policy of deer eradication has taken place in recent years. The lower reaches of this valley were once a marvellous roe forest; now the animals there are almost rare. It is only fair to state that both the Forestry Commission, and a number of the larger estates, have now adopted a more humane system of roedeer control entailing the employment of trained stalkers properly equipped with modern high-velocity rifles fitted with telescopic sights.

In Rothiemurchus and its immediate neighbourhood the situation is entirely different, for here there are places where roedeer have existed in comparative peace since time immemorial. On and around the hill known as Ord Ban, which overlooks Loch an Eilean, there are many roedeer, and in the adjacent birch woods the rings made by these deer during their mating dances must have been in existence before man ever came on the scene.

Roedeer are known to be very territorial in their habits. The males, in particular, will guard their homeland with great pugnacity, and unless they are unduly disturbed, or actually destroyed or beaten up by a stronger buck, they will hold their grounds for years. There are several places in and around Rothiemurchus where bucks have guarded their own domains for year after year; and when they have been shot, or died of old age, one of their descendants has taken over. Such traditional places are to be found around Tullochghru, Whitewells, Achnachoichen, Blackpark and the Croft. This roe zone, as it were, stretches from the Lairig path to the shores of Loch an Eilean.

Then again there are static groups of roe by Moormore, Achnahatnich and Drumintoul, right up to Pityoulish but not beyond. These districts could well be described as a paradise for the roe-lover. It is possible to watch and study these lovely little deer day after day and month after month.

When following the roe one very quickly gets to know the individuals and their particular characteristics. Roedeer, at times, are very vocal animals. There is one old buck who lives in a small area to the south of the stone cottage, which used to be known as Mrs. Cameron's cottage, on the banks of Loch an Eilean. Whenever he is disturbed, by man or beast, he barks—and his bark varies in a noticeable manner, so that it is not difficult to tell what it is that is making him "talk".

Both bucks and does are vocal. Their voice has been likened to that of a Scottish collie dog, and this description is quite apt. That roedeer can communicate with each other by means of their voices there is no doubt. The note most frequently heard by the human ear is the call of alarm or warning. This is uttered, at times, by both sexes. A young buck will bark with a higher-pitched voice than an old one, an old doe may bark gruffly with a sort of grumbling note. Bucks when on the rut can become very vociferous, and they will continue to abuse each other for considerable periods of time as they circle and run about the verges of their various territories.

Both roe does and their kids squeak, and man has contrived little whistles, most of them less than a thumb's length and thickness in size, with which to call these deer. During the time of the mating the call of a kid or a doe is supposed to bring a buck, but unless the human caller is extremely skilful in his imitation of roe-language he may entice a doe who runs to the call-note of her false kid. Some men can bark to a buck and get an answer, and this is not too difficult a feat, particularly when the rut is on. An examination of the language of the roe is only one of the many interests which these animals can provide. Their behaviour and antics, there is no other word for it, during their honeymoon period, are a nature study second to none.

There are places in and around Rothiemurchus which are now the recognised ringing grounds of the roe. The site of a series of such rings in a silver birch wood by the Croft must be of considerable antiquity. This set of rings has been in use for the past forty years, and they were probably used by roe long before that. Some rings are resorted to every summer, and thus they are in fact established places. During the mid-winter months they are nearly always deserted and seldom, if ever, used; but with the approach of the roedeers' rut, which normally occurs in July and early August, the rings are again brought into use. Elsewhere fresh sets of rings are formed, annually, preparatory to the mating period.

The rings made by roedeer are not by any means always circular in shape. They may be oval and they are quite frequently in the form of the figure eight. They nearly always have some sort of a pivot, or pivots, around which the deer course. The centre pieces can vary appreciably; they may consist of a sapling, an old oak, a bunch of tansy or merely a tuft of coarse grass. Symmetry in design is nearly always a feature of the rings. Irregular patterns are the exception. Couches are often to be found near by, for roe will run continuously in their tracks until completely exhausted, when they appear to need immediate rest. The couches, like the rings themselves, are used time and time again.

It has been suggested that it is the female who first deliberately forms the rings or revives the established ones. Some observers believe that it is a combined operation on the part of both the male and the female which creates these well-defined dancing places. It is undoubtedly the oncome of the oestrus in the female which touches off the first annual creation of the rings. When the doe comes in season she becomes skittish—there is no other word for it! Then she begins to play and gambol, and in doing so she seems to select shady, secret places which are the likeliest spots in which these mating rings are to be found. Once a doe is sexually attractive to the buck then the love-dance starts. The doe circles evasively until the love-chase gradually increases in tempo, when a wild rushing around results in circles, ovals or figures of eight. This continues as the mating urge grows until both participants become completely exhausted and resort to their couches. Actual union may take place in the ringing area, but as often as not this happens away from the rings themselves.

Although the rings of the roe are usually only used in July and August, they are undoubtedly sometimes revisited in the autumn, when the so-called erotic rut may occur. This late mating of the roedeer is not, as yet, fully understood, nor is this phenomenon generally accepted, but there is, certainly, some evidence that coupling does take place at this season. When it does occur it is, perhaps, rather natural that it should happen in the original honeymoon sites. It has been suggested that odd young female roes may miss the early oestrus to come in season at a later date, when they become attractive to the males.

The sight of roedeer engaged in their frantic antics in these secret love sites is surely one of the most enthralling, as well as exciting, spectacles which nature is able to provide.

CHAPTER XX

Stoats and Weasels

In Scotland, in the past, the stoat was known as the big weasel or whittret. The weasel was also called a whittret as well as the mouse-weasel, futteret and, surprisingly, game-rat.

There is an old saw which says that a weasel is weasily distinguished from a stoat, which is stoatally different—there is much in this quip. A weasel is much smaller than a stoat, with a shorter tail not tipped with black at the end as it is in the stoat. The weasel's movements are rather inclined to be sinuous, whereas the stoat appears to have a more prancing action. The stoat breeds once a year, the weasel twice. When one is used to seeing the two animals it is easy, even at a quick glance, to differentiate between them.

Many stoats change the colour of their coat to white in winter. This winter pelage is known as "winter ermine", and a good skin used to be highly valued in the fur trade. Nowadays, however, nearly every ermine pelt found in the fur market comes from abroad. British stoats produce aberrant winter pelts, and there is much variety in individuals. The weasel in Britain rarely turns white in winter, although in northern Scandinavia and Siberia weasels frequently change to white.

It has been stated in the past that in the Scottish Highlands most stoats assume a white ermine coat in winter, but this is not correct. At one time William Marshall went to a great deal of trouble to make a collection for a museum of the skins of stoats for every month of the year. Those taken from stoats in the vicinity of Nethybridge in Inverness-shire showed a very wide variation. A similar experiment was carried out by Arthur White, who used to be a keeper at Milton Abbas in Dorset. White's skins, sent to the Natural History Museum in

Scotland has many herds of wild goats

Mikel Ursi who introduced reindeer to Glenmore

On the lower reaches of the Spey

Reindeer are the traditional haulers of Father Christmas's sleigh

Kensington, showed little difference from Marshall's. There appears to be little doubt that there is a considerable difference in the individual's coat-change characteristics, as well as a variance in the actual number of stoats which change colour in different years.

One year may well see more stoats assume a full-white winter pelage than others. The winter of 1960–61 was a case in point; during this winter I received numerous reports of white stoats being seen in places from south Wales to Berwickshire and beyond. One man who was at the time working on rabbit clearance on the Borders reported no less than sixteen pure-white specimens that winter; and he is the type who can be relied upon not to duplicate his seeings. The theory that it is essentially the temperature which determines pelage-change from reddish-brown to white in winter is certainly exploded when one realises that the winter of 1960–61 was an exceptionally mild one throughout the British Isles.

There is something very fascinating about these quick, fierce little carnivores. They appear to have terrific character. To be able to watch either a stoat or weasel when one is unobserved is a most satisfactory pursuit. Both animals are extremely courageous, and at times pugnacious, creatures. They will tackle prey many times their own size and weight. Hares are sometimes killed by stoats; and the capercaillie, which is almost as large as a small turkey, has been known to have been accounted for by a stoat. In this country stoats and weasels have few enemies except man, although some may be killed by foxes, and possibly semi-feral cats.

Both species have powerful stink glands which may render them unattractive to other predators, but neither the stoat nor the weasel uses this weapon of defence to the same extent that the skunk, also a mustelid, does on the American continent. The scent glands of the stoat and the weasel would appear to have largely the function of mutual attraction, perhaps during the breeding season, and not one of offence or defence.

Until quite recently, stoats and weasels have always been

regarded as the game preserver's traditional enemies, and hundreds of them were destroyed annually, mainly in tunnel traps. Numbers are still accounted for by trapping. When the gin-trap was a legal killing device, prior to 1957, many stoats were taken in these contrivances. The banning of the gin, south of the Border, has been a factor in the preservation of the species; although the tunnel trap appears to be a far more effective catcher than the gin for these little mustelids. Weasels were not so often found in gins, presumably because being considerably smaller than stoats, they were able to escape from the traps or perhaps even leave them unsprung.

The value of these small predators as assistants to gamekeepers was realised many years ago by naturalists like Brian Vesey-FitzGerald, who pointed out that where rats were plentiful on a shoot a pair of stoats were far more efficient hunters than a couple of keepers. The planter of trees today realises the value of both the stoat and the weasel in his woodlands; for these animals kill numerous mice and voles, both harmful to the arboriculturist's young trees. Since the planting of trees has assumed such enormous proportions throughout Scotland, its population of both stoats and weasels must have increased considerably during the present century. Woodland areas such as exist in many parts of the country today afford marvellous shelter for such animals.

Like the American mink, a great fisherman—sometimes known in its native country as "the fisher"—both stoats and weasels are excellent aquatics. They do not appear to include fish to any extent in their diet, but they will enter the water quite fearlessly. Both species have been known to swim to islands and to clear them largely of their wild-life.

Sometimes stoats and weasels form packs of their own kind in order to hunt. Whether these packs are families or a collection of families is anyone's guess. These little killers always seem to pursue their quarry by scent. To watch them engaged in tracking their prey is rather like seeing a pack of miniature hounds engaged in following the line of a fox or a hare.

Stoats and Weasels

There is a story, which has now become almost a legend, of a postman on Speyside who was pursued by a pack of stoats or weasels. Their actual identity does not appear to have been entirely established. Early in the morning, whilst on his rounds in the country delivering the mail, he came upon a number of these animals on the hunt. When the leading animal saw the postie he made for him, followed by his many little relatives. The G.P.O.'s representative turned and fled in terror, and that is the end of the story.

Rather surprisingly, because both the stoat and the weasel are such quick, active creatures, they are not by any means rare road casualties. Both animals haunt the highways for the dead birds and beasts killed on them by our fast-moving traffic; it is when they are engaged in their quest for such easy meat, and they become careless, that they themselves get run over.

Walking one day along the road from Inverdruie to Coylum Bridge, I saw a dead she-stoat lying by the grass verge. She was a road casualty. Beside the corpse there was a tiny baby stoat who was trying to suckle the still warm body of its dam. Returning along the same road half an hour later, I could find no evidence of this recent tragedy. That another stoat, or stoats, had removed the corpse and its young, is likely. Both stoats and weasels are known to be attracted by their moribund kind. Many instances have been recorded of these animals carrying their own dead, but whether they will bury their deceased is not known; although this is possible, for larger members of the mustelid family have been observed to do so. Dr. Ernest Neal has fully recorded a badger's burial in his world-famed book on this animal. Badgers are also mustelids.

The old-time Highland keepers were well aware of the propensity of both stoats and weasels for their own deceased, and it was quite usual for these game guardians to bait their traps with the corpse of a dead stoat or weasel.

CHAPTER XXI

The Brown Hare and the Blue Hare

The long, wide valley of the Spey and its high hinterlands contain both British species of hare—the lowland brown hare, *Lepus europaeus occidentalis*, and the highland blue hare, *Lepus timidus scoticus*. The former, which is the bigger animal, is seldom found at any great altitude, whilst the latter appears to prefer heights. Certainly the blue hare, or arctic hare, is more rabbit-like to look at than the brown. The main difference, perhaps, apart from its structure, is the fact that the blue has a decided colour moult every year. Moults would be the more correct word, for the blue hare is believed to undergo three moults a year, whilst the brown hare only goes through two.

The blue hare which is, in summer, a sort of blue-grey dusky-brown, turns to nearly pure white in winter. In between times, during the spring and autumn, the blue's pelt can assume the most surprising combinations of brown, grey and white which, at times, gives it a piebald or skewbald appearance. On the other hand, the brown hare is much more conservative in its coat-changes, as both in winter and summer, this animal is largely reddish brown with whitish underparts and yellowish legs.

Some years ago I was sent a skin by William Marshall of an alleged brown-blue hare hybrid. The ears were shorter than those of the normal brown hare, the colour along the back certainly resembled the bluish grey of a blue hare in summer coat, and there was not the usual black patch on the upper surface of the tail which is a characteristic of the brown hare. The circumstances of this hybrid's creation were convincing. The trapper who gave it to Marshall had an area of young conifers in his care which was completely wired in. He had successfully eliminated most of the hares within the area, though he knew of a brown doe hare which was still about. During the snow a blue hare from higher up in the hill country got in, and in the following spring these two were seen "on the go" together. The skin was perhaps naturally thought to be the result of the union of this pair, as it was killed some months later when any leverets would be full grown. As it turned out, the skin, although it is a rather unusual one for a brown hare, has proved to be that of a normal brown hare, *Lepus europaeus occidentalis*. This is the verdict of Dr. Corbet of the Natural History Museum in Kensington, London, and also of Mr. Ray Hewson of Keith, Banffshire, who is regarded today as our greatest expert on the blue, or mountain hare, *Lepus timidus scoticus*.

Authenticated evidence of a cross between a blue hare and a brown hare is somewhat scanty, although there is plenty in literature about the existence of these hybrids. J. G. Millais always regarded them as fairly common, and in his book *The Mammals of Great Britain and Ireland* he says that the two species frequently interbred. On one occasion he mentions that between ten and twelve were shot in a drive at Murthly in Perthshire. On another day's hare shooting, this time at Barnside in the same county, seventy-two brown hares were shot, twenty-eight blue hares and no less than six hybrids.

Archibald Thorburn, the great animal and bird artist, confirms what Millais wrote, and in his *British Mammals* he says: "The mountain hare does not always keep to his hilly fastnesses, but will often come down to the lower ground in hard weather and when it meets the brown hare on the lower levels the two species will interbreed."

Old copies of *The Naturalist* indicate that the blue hare–brown hare cross was quite a popular topic in the nineteenth century, as was also the alleged hare–rabbit hybrid. But the evidence published in nearly every case of these rare creatures rather tends to show that the specimens taken, or seen, may well have been normal blue hares in partial moult, when they can assume the most astonishing coat colours. A blue hare recently observed in the spring in the valley of Spey near Kingussie, was like a skewbald pony, being a sort of rich brown with occasional white spots along the back and rump.

Mammalogists of the present century, in their various works, do not say much about the existence or possibility of this cross. Dr. Lonnburg of the Zoological Museum, Uppsala, has published a paper on this subject in which he maintains that hybrid hares are comparatively common in southern Sweden owing to the increased introduction of brown hares into the country for sport.

To the layman who has had an opportunity of studying both species in their natural habitats over a long period of years, it is perhaps rather surprising that more proven cases of hybridism between blue and brown hares do not occur. We now know quite definitely that the antagonism between the two species does not really exist, and that their segregation is largely a matter of habitat preference.

The two hares, brown and blue, are in many respects remarkably alike in their play, way of life and food intake. Blue and brown eat the same food during the winter months in many a Scottish glen. Because overlapping of territory is not at all uncommon, and these two hares are often in each other's territories, one might expect a great deal more intermarriage. There is certainly no proof that the brown and the blue hare will never mix their blood, but it looks equally sure that intermarriage of these two hares with a successful outcome is extremely rare. Dr. Corbet says that of the many skins of reputed hybrids in the collection of the Natural History Museum, none could be said to be undisputed, and some, at least, would appear to be those of aberrant brown hares.

CHAPTER XXII

Wild Goats

During the earlier part of the present century there existed in what is now the Glenmore National Park a flourishing herd of wild goats. One fierce winter an avalanche struck the herd to destroy it completely; there were no survivors. There are few people alive today who knew of the existence of these wild goats of the high places. William Marshall was one man who knew them. The golgotha of this herd, he used to say, was in Coire Lochan, not far from the ski-lift and now a favourite spot for visiting hill-climbers.

Very occasionally one may see a solitary wandering wild goat in the district. The odd beast has been seen in Coire Beinne and the dense juniper thickets of Coire Buidh, but these are likely to be wanderers who have, at some time or other, hived off from the larger herds now in existence in other parts of the Cairn Gorm range, such as the herd of Lochnagar in Aberdeenshire. It is perhaps strange that hardy, mountainous animals like these feral goats can be destroyed by the elements, but the Coire Lochan disaster is not by any means unique, for herds in other places, such as the Cheviot hills, have been utterly destroyed by excessive snowfalls and avalanches.

Scotland has many herds of wild goats, from the lowlands of Galloway to the high, bleak uplands of Caithness. Until quite recently there was a small herd at Lethendry Voil, in the lower Monadhliaths; these animals were in the habit of coming right down to the main railway line which now runs from Aviemore to Inverness. A few miles farther north, a thriving herd existed just north of Carrbridge, by the main road to Inverness. Remnants of this herd, which was severely reduced during the 1939–45 war, are still occasionally to be seen in the foothills south of

Lochindorb. The herd of Beum A'Chaildheimh contains some remarkably fine specimens. Amongst this lot is a big male as white as a Highland wedder; there are others of a brindled grey and brown. The large billies all carry horns which mostly sweep down below their withers.

Most wild goats are extremely hairy creatures, and in a full feral state their coats grow, presumably as a protective measure, right down to their fetlocks. Surprisingly, as a contradiction to the thick-coat-protective theory, the kids, when born in February—often the harshest month of all the year—carry very short coats.

I watched a kid at Lethendry Voil which was a tawny colour almost like that of the true wild goats of the high sierras of southern Europe and Spain—the ibex, which is believed to be the ancestor of all goats. This colour may have been a throw-back to the original species; another characteristic of reversion to type is in the horns of some of the males which resemble, in a remarkable manner, those of the Spanish ibex. There is a case in the Natural History Museum in Kensington, which contains a stuffed ibex shot by the late King Alfonso of Spain. Placed alongside the head of this animal the horns of a big Scottish wild goat show a quite remarkable resemblance.

The British wild goat is named by the scientists as *Capra hircus*; it is the descendant of domestic animals which have, at some time or another, escaped to become wild animals, and in this process many of them have reverted to type, hence the similar horn structure and the original coloration of some of the kids.

No one knows when goats were first brought to the British Isles, for this was a pre-historic event. It is possible that they may have been conveyed here by the Phoenicians, from the Mediterranean countries, who bartered them with the British natives for gold, silver, pearls and the skins of wild animals. Goats were never indigenous to the British Isles. We know this as no fossilised caprine remains have ever been unearthed here. The Mediterranean species, introduced by man, was likely to

Strathspey contains a veritable meshwork of little burns

A box with a glass bottom is useful when fishing for pearls

Pearl fisher's camp

Swift running mountain stream

A large part of the Highland Folk Museum houses domestic articles

Soay sheep, or the sheep of St. Kilda

have been a semi-domesticated animal useful for its milk, skin and flesh. The present herds of Scottish wild goats are the descendants of escapees, but when their ancestors were first freed it is impossible to say. It is also possible that goats may have arrived in this country during the Neolithic period, as their remains have been discovered with those of stone-age man.

Our Scottish wild goats have now evolved a pattern of life not unlike that of our red deer. The master billies come to rut in late October, whilst the nannies kid in February. During the mating period fierce fights may take place between the contending males, when even death may result. An old female, usually with a kid at foot, appears to act as guardian to the herd, for matriarchy is the rule amongst these feral ungulates as it is with the wild red deer. Some naturalists believe that the kidding in February helps to control numbers as this is the year's worst period and comparatively few youngsters survive the winter. The wild goat, unlike the red deer, has never been regarded as a particularly desirable beast of the chase, although most wild goats are wary and not easy to approach. The majority will flee at man's approach or when they get a puff of his wind.

However, there are a few historical references to the hunting of these animals. John Colquhoun of Luss, has recorded in his delightful book *The Moor and the Loch*, published in 1878, the pursuit of the wild goats of Crap-na-Gower, an island in Loch Lomond, and he states that these animals provided excellent sport for the stalker. Crap-na-Gower in the Gaelic means the hill of the goats.

Another interesting account of the wild goat as a hunted animal is to be found in *The Gentleman's Recreation* (1874) by one Nicholas Cox. The author has written: "Alhallowtide is the chiefest Season for Hunting Wild-Goats, observing very well before you Hunt, the advantages of the Coasts, the Rocks and the Places where Goats do lie."

In the present century, the late Frank Wallace has left a

remarkable record of the stalking of wild goats in Sutherland in his book *A Highland Gathering* published in 1932.

A few of these interesting semi-feral creatures, set at large on the hills above Glenmore, and perhaps in the great glen of Einich and the Lairig Pass, might prove a welcome amenity to the many naturalists and visitors who now come in their ever-increasing numbers to these wild, lovely places.

The reindeer, to be dealt with in the next chapter, has been introduced to the National Park; there must surely be sufficient space for *Capra hircus*, an animal of considerable ancestry and interest.

CHAPTER XXIII

Rangifer Tarandus

Beside the steep, twisting, asphalt road which leads from Loch Morlich to the ski-lift in the Glenmore National Park, there is a big notice board bearing the words BEWARE REINDEER. This warning does not mean that *Rangifer tarandus* is a savage beast liable to attack travellers. It is merely advice that the motorist, bound for the high places, should be on the alert so as not to risk collision with one of these free-roaming, bovine-looking cervids. Reindeer now frequent the roadsides on the slopes of the Cairn Gorm mountains for the delicacies they can pick up in the form of rejected sandwiches, chocolate and the other edible matter which has been littered along man's roadways by his passing. The sign BEWARE REINDEER can be placed in the same category as the more frequent notices, posted beside unfenced highways, which warn the motorist that sheep may be on the road.

It is perhaps strange that probably more visitors to the Scottish Highlands have seen these recently-introduced deer than the far more graceful and beautiful red deer, a native of these islands, who carries the proud specific title of *Cervus elaphus scoticus*.

In the popular press, at least, reindeer have lately received far more publicity than our indigenous red deer. There is, of course, an aura of romance about these somewhat placid, semi-domesticated, cattle-like deer. There is also their close association with Christmas and St. Nicholas. Reindeer are the traditional haulers of Father Christmas's gift-laden sleigh; although it must be admitted that today St. Nicholas, the patron saint of Christmas, may just as well arrive down one's false chimney by parachute ejected from a space capsule or in some atomic rocket. The manufacturers of greeting cards have certainly rather soft-pedalled, of recent years, on deer and sleighs, and instead have turned towards more explosive methods of sky-propulsion.

That reindeer should be the drawers of St. Nicholas's sleigh is certainly appropriate, because St. Nicholas is a patron saint of Russia, where his fame lies largely in the legend that he was wont to press little gifts, like nuts and sweets, on children at the festive season, and also because, in the northern regions of the vast continent of Russia, there are many reindeer, both wild and domesticated.

That the reindeer was once an indigenous British animal there is no doubt, and in the past they were possibly far more numerous in Britain than the red deer or roe. The presence of great quantities of the bones and horns of reindeer in bogs, caverns, caves and quarries suggests that they were perhaps the most abundant of all deer in prehistoric times. Like the now extinct wolf and brown bear, there is a legendary record of the reindeer's elimination here, at the hand of man, for the Orcanian Sagas tell of the hunters Ragnald and Harald who came from the Isle of Orkney to hunt the reins of Caithness on the Scottish mainland. This happened towards the middle of the twelfth century, and Britain was then reindeerless until the early 1800s when a certain Robert Traill brought two bulls and a cow reindeer from Archangel to Caithness. This attempt at colonisation failed, almost certainly due to the paucity of numbers introduced, which did not allow for possible casualties.

Later, an early Earl of Fyfe introduced some reindeer into his deer forests of Mar. This experiment also eventually failed, because it was believed that the more virile native red deer in the hills rejected the foreigners by continuously harrying them. Another Scottish nobleman also tried to establish reindeer on his lands. This was the then Duke of Atholl, a great introducer in his time, for he brought to Scotland such animals as reindeer, buffalo and fallow deer. Only the fallow deer have survived, and they are now quite numerous in the woodlands about Blair Atholl. The Duke also brought in to his forests a number of Red Indians. These were to tend the buffalo. The Indians' acquired liking for Scottish mutton, however, eventually led to their elimination from the Highland scene.

The presence of reindeer, in the country surrounding the ski-lift at Glenmore, is mainly of interest because this latest attempt to bring reindeer back to Britain has at last succeeded. The Reindeer Council of the British Isles, who sponsored this experiment in reintroducing *Rangifer tarandus*, did so, in the first instance, shortly after the 1939–45 war; at that time we were extremely short of meat, and also without the financial resources to buy it abroad. Surely, they argued, in the reindeer there was a vast potential for the raising of stock on high mountainous stretches, and on some of our uninhabited Western Islands, where even our native deer and our hardy hill sheep could not eke out an existence. Reindeer are credited, at times, with being able not only to survive but actually to thrive on mosses and lichen!

There is no doubt that the Reindeer Council have met with many difficulties in the introduction of their charges here, and also in their acclimatisation. Obstacles such as long periods of quarantine, and the preliminary keeping of free-roaming beasts in confined quarters, were only some of the early trials which had to be faced. By the time a herd was safely established in the Glenmore area, however, the acute national meat shortage had passed, and it had also become evident that reindeer farming, on the lines of the north Scandinavian and Finnish procedures, was strictly not for us. Reindeer in these countries and elsewhere abroad are substitutes for cattle and sheep, for they provide meat, milk and leather. Their flesh is quite excellent, and is considered to be highly nutritious and easily digested. In Scotland, an intended economic asset has eventually turned out to be mostly an amenity convenience and a curiosity for those many hundreds of tourists who now visit the Glenmore area throughout the summer and winter.

Amongst the reins in Glenmore there is at least one animal

who can draw a sleigh. This is surely worth knowing, for accidents happen, and should Prancer, Dancer, Dasher, Vixen, Comet, Cupid, Donner and Blixen, all permanent members of St. Nicholas's sleigh team, drop out there is now a spare leg, as it were, available to assist in haulage work up in the high hills of the Scottish Highlands.

CHAPTER XXIV

Swift Running Mountain Streams

The search for new waters in which to fish can be a pleasant occupation. When one takes out one's fishing tackle to try for a fish of any sort, be it the little brown trout of the mountain streams, or some specimen salmon from the lower reaches of Spey, one is searching with physical aids for one's quarry. The exploration, and then preparation, before venturing on fresh fishing grounds, can be almost as satisfactory and even as exciting an adventure as the first cast one eventually makes on a new stream or loch perhaps never fished before.

One could spend a lifetime building up a library of angling books. More than two thousand volumes have been written on the family *salmonidae* alone—this family includes both salmon and trout. There are books of the reminiscent sort and those which endeavour to instruct one how to engage in the so-called art of the angle. There are guide books which tell you where to go, the price of your fishing and the sport you are likely to obtain. Such works are best typified by *Where to Fish*, which is published periodically by the Field Press. This book, in its latest edition, is very nearly an encyclopaedia for the questing angler.

If you have not the time or means to build up an angling library of your own, there is always the public library. Here on the shelves, usually labelled *Sports and Pastimes*, you will certainly discover a number of volumes which will aid you in your search for fresh waters to resort to on an angling vacation. As far as Strathspey is concerned there is no better guide book than the recently published work by James Coutts entitled *Game Fishing*. A publication of the Highland Development Board, this little manual is very modestly priced, and contains within its covers a wealth of information about the fishing available in most parts of Inverness-shire.

Maps hold a great fascination for many of us. The scrutiny of a large-scale ordinance map of a territory to be visited can afford one infinite pleasure. The examination of the tributaries and waterways, as well as the sites of hundreds of lochs, will quickly indicate that there are miles upon miles of virgin streams and hidden lochans where possibly man has yet to cast a fly.

When you want to go away for a time on a fishing holiday to some new place you have read of, or heard about, then you have to find out how to get to your destination. Should you decide to go by train, even looking up the A.B.C. can be a pleasurable occupation. If you have a car, the A.A. yellow guide, or the blue R.A.C. one, will almost certainly have to be consulted for the nearest town or hotel convenient to your sport. Routes will have to be explored, and then comes the final practical preparation of your fishing tackle, and the decision about just what to take and what to leave at home.

Nowadays the cult of the angling course is steadily increasing. Coutts refers to them in *Game Fishing*. The specific course he mentions is conducted by A.B.W. Ltd. of Great Britain at the Aviemore Centre. Fly- and bait-casting are covered, the first steps of which are taught from casting platforms on the shores of two small lochs within the grounds of the Centre. From here the pupil will progress to the banks of the river Spey, where bank-fishing for trout and salmon follow. As with all instructional courses the emphasis is on casting proficiency rather than taking fish—the first leads to the second. The cost of this course is about five guineas, which includes lectures and film shows.

This Aviemore Centre course is only one of many which are now being regularly conducted in various parts of the Highlands.

Among the more attractive forms of Highland angling is the ever available pursuit of that universal and sporting little game fish the brown trout, *Salmo trutta*, in some sparkling river or, more likely, lively mountain stream. There is something particularly fascinating about a quick, animated little burn as it twists, turns and falls from its source high up in some hill, eventually to join some larger waterway. Mountain burns never seem the same on two consecutive days, for by their nature they are ever-changing. A spate will come and go in a few hours, and in the summer the water may well shrink till one wonders how a trout could survive in its stagnant shallows.

To fish a mountain burn is always an adventure. The element of surprise in this kind of fishing is considerable. One never knows what to expect just around the next corner. No two pools are entirely alike, and because there are so many little burns, as compared to big rivers, their variety is great. There is plenty of exercise, too, in this form of sport, as the width of most hill burns is small so that you can travel fairly quickly along their courses, approaching each bend and pool with care before testing them with your bait. The mountain trout fisher will cover many miles in a day's angling.

Mountain burns are nearly always animated places occupied not only by fish but by birds and beasts as well. Wild deer know that succulent feeding is to be found within the burn's way, and water-voles and water-shrews make use of its bed. Dippers, sandpipers, herons and ring ouzels frequent the rocks and banks of most highland waterways, so that should the fish not be taking there is much to hold the angler's interest.

Of all the ways of fishing little rivers, my own preference is up-river-worming, because this particular type of fishing is an artful game requiring a hunter's skill. Mountain burns are frequently wind-swept places, and it is often possible to fish successfully with a worm, when a fly could scarcely be got on to the water and particularly on just the spot where a fish is likely to lie. Up-river-worming requires the finest of tackle, for during the greater part of the time one is fishing the water of these hill burns is quite transparent. Some lead-shot on the line is nearly always advisable in this form of angling, and the number of pellets used will vary with the state of the water, for a spate will need more shot than a near-dry river bed.

There are no qualifications as to rods; some up-river-wormers prefer short, stiff rods, whilst others go for long, whippy ones. Up-river-worming is very much a matter of each man to his own choice.

One tedious part of this form of angling is the constant need to thread one's hook. Most worms are fragile, and although there are various means by which they may be somewhat toughened no worm lasts for ever. In an attempt to overcome this nuisance I once invested in an imitation rubber worm artistically mounted on Stewart tackle. To the human eye the thing was as worm-like as makes no matter; to the trout it must have appeared entirely false for no fish ever rose to this sham lure.

It is really surprising what excellent baskets can be had from the little streams of the hills and uplands. The average size of fish may not be great; a half-pounder is a prize and should one be so fortunate as to take six such fish from a mountain burn this surely is enough, for it is not substantially the fish that makes hill-trout fishing so attractive, it is the scene, the stalk, the climb, the excitement of exploration and the sight of wild birds, beasts and even flying insects—for what could be more lovely than a sky-blue dragonfly in shimmering summer sunlight—which all combine to make the fishing of mountain waters one of the more attractive forms of angling.

The fly-fisherman, both wet and dry, may profess to scorn the worm, but those who have tried up-river-worming on a Highland burn will admit its attraction; and in the angling world the truth is that more men fish with the worm than with the fly!

Every angler, of course, has his own particular preference for the sort of water in which he likes to fish. Some men love the breadth and power of great rivers like the Tay, the Tweed, the Spey and the Dee from which to take a lordly salmon. Others prefer the placid waters of some ancient, still canal on which to contemplate a float. But the swift, singing, mountain burn narrow enough to leap across from bank to bank has a fascination all its own.

Strathspey and its high hinterlands contain a veritable mesh-work of little burns and rivers, some of them, as yet, quite unexplored. James Coutts in his *Game Fishing* briefly mentions some of these, but half the fun of angling in mountain streams is the preliminary search for likely places, and their eventual exploration with rod and line. It is no exaggeration at all to say that in the regions with which this book is mainly concerned there are hundreds of miles of tributary waters, nearly all of which contain *Salmo trutta*, the lovely brown trout of the Highlands.

CHAPTER XXV

The Pearls of Spey

It was tedious work splitting the mussel-shells and then squeezing with a thumb amongst the slime of the two halves to feel if there was a pearl there. It must have been the memory of that lovely glistening orb in the window of the little jeweller's shop in Grantown-on-Spey, priced at £20, which kept us going. The pearl in the shop window was the size of a large pea, with a lovely sheen about it which somehow reminded one of sunlight breaking through the mist over the distant Grampian mountains.

Although the shelling was monotonous work, it was pleasant there on the banks of the big river, watching the swift-running water on its way down to Speymouth and the North Sea. There had been no rain for ten days, so that the water was low and so clear that it was quite easy to distinguish the mussels from the stones on the river's bottom.

We were wearing bathing shorts, and had waded into the river in search of the mussel-beds. The water was cold to the feet and legs, coming as it did from the patches of snow which still lay scattered on the high tops of the surrounding hills. The brilliant hot sun, however, helped to keep the rest of our bodies warm. It had not been long before we had found the shells, and then we had worked them loose from the bed of the stream with our toes, or with a cleft stick. After a short while we had gathered fifty mussels and we began the shelling.

Freshwater pearls are by no means entirely confined to Scotland, because they are to be found in the majority of rivers and other stretches of water, such as ponds and lakes, throughout the British Isles. However, the pearls of this country are usually referred to as "Scottish" pearls by the trade so as to distinguish them from the oriental pearls of sea-origin which may come from as far away as the Gulf of Arabia or the west coast of Australia. Usually mussels taken from fast-running British rivers are more likely to produce good-quality pearls than those from shells found in stagnant waters.

There are a number of ways of fishing for freshwater pearls; you can wade in and feel with your toes, as we did, but wading can be cold work after a time, and the professional pearlers of the past were in the habit of using coracles or small flat-bottomed punt-like boats, usually attached to a rope which was handled by a partner standing on the river bank. By using a wooden box with a built-in glass bottom the man in the boat could search the river-bed for the mussels. A box with a glass bottom is also useful when wading, particularly when the surface of the water is being rippled by the wind; the glass resting on the water's surface tends to eliminate all surface distortion and allows the pearler to distinguish objects on the river-bed quite distinctly.

Most pearlers nowadays use a gripping stick both when wading or fishing from a boat. The stick can be of any length so long as it is sufficient to reach to the depth of the mussel-bed, but the diameter should be about that of an ordinary walking-stick with a split end to it where the ferrule is usually found. With this split-stick it is quite easy to disengage the mussel shells from their beds; for the freshwater mussel is not a particularly securely seated creature. When a mussel-bed is discovered it should never, under any circumstances, be entirely stripped. Only a limited number of the larger and older shells should be taken; the lesser shells should always be left as a breeding stock. Further, these smaller shells are not so likely to contain pearls as are the larger specimens. The professional pearlers of old were well aware of this commonsense fact.

A pearl, strangely enough, is a form of imperfection in an otherwise normal bivalve. The intrusion into the living mussel of some extraneous substance is believed to cause irritation to the interior. In self-defence the mollusc coats this irritant with layers of nacre, or mother-of-pearl, which is the normal iridescent lining of the shell itself.

The pearl mussel, *Unio margaritifer*, was known in the past by such varied names as the pond mussel, the swan mussel, the pearl mussel and the painter's mussel. The painter's mussel was so-called because its shells were frequently used for holding watercolour paints.

The big swan mussel may attain a width of over seven inches. These molluscs are long-lived, and some scientists have even suggested that individuals may live as long as a century. The freshwater mussel of our British lakes, ponds and rivers is estimated to produce over a million eggs. The parent mussels retain their ova until they are hatched in a larval stage. The glochidia, as they are called, are then ejected, and attach themselves to the gills of fishes, such as trout, roach, perch and sticklebacks, who carry them on their ventral fins until they are shed in other parts of the stream or lake. The shell develops whilst still being carried by the fish, and the young mussels eventually drop to the bottom to form fresh colonies. This process of propagation is in some ways similar to the known method whereby wading birds carry both frog-spawn and fish-spawn on their legs to new waters to reproduce the species.

Although pearl-fishing in Scotland has today virtually ceased on a commercial basis, there is little doubt that in the seventeenth century the Scottish pearl industry was of some importance. Still further back in history we find that Pliny, the famed Roman naturalist and historian, has left a record in one of his many books, *Historia Naturalis*, that the freshwater pearls of Britain are amongst its most important exportable commodities.

One day when I was in Edinburgh, I went up to the Castle to look at the Scottish Crown Jewels, a very fine display. The Crown of Scotland contains no less than seven pearls found in mussels from Scottish waters. Every one of these seven pearls measures over a quarter of an inch in diameter, so that these may be regarded as exceptional gems. However, whilst I was examining these pearls the attendant in the jewel room in the Castle casually mentioned that a lady had visited the Castle not long ago and had brought with her a pearl, recently taken from a West Highland river, which was a far finer and bigger specimen than any in the Crown of Scotland!

Our own pearl-fishing expedition on the Spey yielded no such priceless gems, but rather surprisingly perhaps, we did find three small pink seed-pearls, which were duly placed in a match-box lined with cotton wool—quite valueless trivia, but still most exciting and pleasant in their discovery.

CHAPTER XXVI

Phantoms and Black Dogs

The Cairn Gorm National Nature Reserve contains its own particular phantoms, of which the most famous is undoubtedly the Grey Man of Ben Macdhui. The Grey Man has a number of alternate names, such as the Grey Man of the Lairig and the Big Grey Man. There is also his Gaelic title of Fear Liath Mor. I have never seen or heard the Grey Man, but others have.

One has to concede that there must be something there when men of undoubted veracity and reputation like the late Professor J. N. Collie and Dr. Julius Kellas, who later lost his life when climbing Everest, both claimed to have seen the Grey Man. These men were members of the old Cairn Gorm Club, and accustomed to spend a good deal of their time in the hills climbing and walking. The Cairn Gorm Club was a sort of pioneer mountaineering group formed of people who loved the hills and the exploration of them. Seton Gordon mentions Fear Liath Mor in his article in *Country Life* of October 28th, 1967, and he writes that the noise of the Big Grey Man's gigantic footsteps brought terror to the heart of a celebrated mountaineer. This was presumably Kellas.

One day when I was discussing Highland phantoms and ghosts with the late William Marshall, he told me that although he did not believe in these things he had, on one occasion, known great fear when out alone in the hills. He had climbed up the Lurcher which lies above the Lairig, or Grey Pass, and was walking parallel with the path well below him. It had been a day of fitful sunshine with a good deal of low cloud hanging about. A high wind would occasionally blow wisps of cloud across the face of the Lurcher and over the corrie below towards Braeriach. Marshall had reached the summit of the Lurcher, and after pausing for a brief rest to enjoy a temporary break in the clouds, which had brought the sunshine, he set off again towards the Wells of Dee on the Aberdeenshire side of the pass.

Almost at once he felt he was being followed. He had not seen anything, but that something was there on the open empty scree he was certain. He was not frightened at first, but rather curious. He began to walk a little faster; the noise of following footsteps grew louder. It was like someone shadowing him. The quicker he went, the more fearful the atmosphere became. He got home quite safely, but the sensations he had experienced that day up on the Lurcher have been those of others of us who have been so fortunate as to have been able to spend some time in the high lovely places.

I cannot claim to have seen the Grey Man, but I have been lucky enough to have witnessed an almost parallel apparition. This was in Badenoch. The man who was with me at the time was George Kennedy, who was then the head stalker at Drui-machder. George Kennedy's granddaughter Margaret is now the wife of Bill McHardy, the stalker at Gaick. Kennedy and I were after an old stag on the western flank of the Boar of Badenoch, that famous rounded hill which towers over the Pass of Druimachder, and through which so many motorists pass today. The phenomenon has been spoken of as the Spectre of the Boar, and it is supposed to be a gigantic figure which shows itself on certain occasions, and under certain conditions, on the skyline.

George Kennedy and I had set out from the lodge at Drui-machder at nine o'clock. We had gone up the pony track which leads to the summit of the Boar, as this was a likely place to find a stag. It was a day of low cloud which had prevented us from making for the high tops above Loch Ericht. We found an old beast with rather a poor head below the rim of the Boar, and decided to stalk him. We left the ponyman on the path with the deer pony, telling him to wait until he heard the shot and then to come on. It was not a difficult stalk, as the wind was right and there was plenty of cover. The only snag was that the low cloud would occasionally fill the corrie, blotting out our quarry.

We were within 400 yards of where we thought the lone stag was when I felt Kennedy prod me in the back with his staff. I froze instantly, thinking that he had seen the stag. Instead he pointed towards the skyline of the Boar along which wisps of cloud were scudding. There, in huge silhouette, was the figure of a man striding forward through the cloud wrack. The figure was about twelve feet high, and much larger than any human being. As the cloud cleared the figure seemed to vanish. Rather to my surprise, Kennedy said that it was now no use following up our stag. I insisted, and we went forward. During the first clear period we searched in vain for the stag we were after, but he had evidently completely vanished. Kennedy said the Spectre would have put him off; I think this was likely, as the apparition we had seen that day was remarkably "alive".

The explanation of the Spectre of the Boar is, I think, quite a mundane one. It is the identical phenomenon to that experienced by many travellers in aeroplanes, and particularly those of us who have flown in the older, lower-flying machines. The sun throws the shadow of the moving plane against a background of cloud or mist. The figure of one of us, probably myself as I was leading, was thrown by the sun against the racing clouds above. The movement of the clouds themselves seemed to accelerate the pace of the shadow. I have often wondered whether this is not the explanation of the occasional occurrences of the Grey Man of the Lairig Ghru—but then there are the footsteps. The silence during Kennedy's and my vision was complete.

There is a lesser-known phantom in the National Nature Reserve. This is the black dog of Loch Einich. Seton Gordon knows something of this legend, but he has written that he has never seen the black dog which is supposed to haunt the neighbourhood of the upper bothy which is now nothing but a tumble of stones. Seton Gordon stayed in this bothy, before it was burnt down, for some three weeks in summer after the first world war; so that he certainly had a full opportunity to see any dogs if they were about.

CHAPTER XXVII

Highland Folk Museum

The eight o'clock weather forecast on the B.B.C was not encouraging. It had suggested a day of persistent rain with, possibly, occasional bright periods later in the day. By eleven o'clock there was no sign whatsoever of a break in the clouds. It was certainly a suitable day on which to visit Am Fasgadh, the Highland Folk Museum at Kingussie. Started by Miss I. F. Grant as a private enterprise, the museum and its contents were purchased by the Pilgrim Trust who have now handed it over to the four Scottish Universities of Aberdeen, Edinburgh, Glasgow and St. Andrews to administer.

The township of Kingussie, usually pronounced King-eussie, has a considerable history of its own. From the earliest times it has been a centre of habitation. The early Iberians settled here. The Picts used and fortified the mound of Ruthven across the Spey. It is possible that the Romans may have had a camp and worked the silver mines in the vicinity.

The museum premises consist of a pleasant, white-harled, early Victorian residence, and a number of modern annexes made necessary as a result of recent acquisitions. The fact that the main exhibits are housed, as it were, in a private residence is rather an added attraction, for there is none of the sombre dullness all too frequently to be found in some of our older museums. Am Fasgadh is the Gaelic for The Shelter. A suitable name, surely, for a Highland Folk Museum, for it shelters, in reality, the material remains of a way of life which has gone for ever.

The creation of this project has not been an easy task. Inspired by the pride in their past of the peoples of Scandinavia, who had developed the idea of the folk museum, Miss I. F.

Grant set out to organise a similar institution in the Highlands of Scotland. After a disheartening start in a disused church in the island of Iona off the coast of Mull, the collection was moved to Laggan. While it was at Laggan the 1939 war started, and this meant a period of arrested development. In 1944, however, the exhibition was opened to the public in its present premises. Fortunately, around the house itself, which is within sight of the main railway line from Perth to Inverness, there is sufficient ground to contain actual specimens of the old dwellings in which our ancestors lived. In the past there used to be, in the fields around these ancient houses, a number of Soay sheep, or the sheep of St. Kilda's. The wool of these sheep is a deep, rich, chocolate brown; and although not as primitive as the original mouflon of Sardinia these animals appear somewhat similar in type. The great massive horns and the very pronounced Roman nose closely resemble those of the true wild sheep. The Soay sheep, however, inhabit the precincts of Am Fasgadh no more.

The exact replicas of some of the old dwellings are, from an architectural aspect, extremely interesting. To ensure exactitude, one of the island crofters' homes on view was erected *in situ* under the personal supervision of an old man who came over for this purpose from the Isle of Lewis. The lack of height of this building is particularly noticeable until one realises that, in the outer islands, where gales are frequent and there is little shelter, only a low-built dwelling could stand up to the weather. The squat house, in fact, was the only way of being able to keep a roof above one's head. To keep the interior of the place dry double walls were built with a core of sand in between. The roof timbers rest on the inner wall, thus permitting the rainwater to percolate through the core of sand.

A rather more recent mason-built "but-and-ben", of the type once widely met with on the mainland, has also been erected in the grounds. This "housie" has fireplaces and chimney flues in each gable. It is fascinating to be able to enter these facsimiles of the ancient houses in which the Scots of the past dwelt, and to be able to explore and examine their construction.

Within the museum itself there are many items of interest for the naturalist and sportsman as well as the historian. One wing of the house contains examples of locally-produced textiles and linens. Primitive looms, spinning wheels, wool combs, spindles, cords and implements for scutching flax are shown.

A selection of particular interest to the botanist is a display of plant-dyes used in the colouring of tartan cloths. Full-scale watercolour paintings, to which are attached specimens of the vegetable matter used in the dyes, illustrate the astonishing variety of dye-stuffs which were available for the purpose of colouring the threads and wool which went to make up a piece of cloth. Alder bark, charlock, sloe, ragwort, marigold, water-lily, peat, fern, tansy, bell heather, elm, thistle, bracken, rowanberry and various lichens are only a sample of what is on view. In order to obtain stability in the dye, alum was frequently used. The tinted fabrics were then boiled so as to fix the colour. Samples of some of the old tartan cloths are shown to demonstrate the skill of the weaver. The blend of colours in a number of these cloths is a fine tribute to the taste of the original creators.

A large part of the museum houses domestic articles. All of these items are interesting, and they are certainly splendid advertisements of the skilful manner in which the local inhabitants of the past were able to utilise the material available for their domestic requirements. Brooms and brushes were made of heather twigs, rushes, bent-grass and even moss. Ropes were woven of horse-hair, rushes and heather fronds as well as the roots of trees and shrubs.

In one section there are beautiful examples of home-made wooden vessels fashioned from birch and fir. On the west coast of Scotland, due to the scarcity of timber, scrub was often resorted to as a substitute for wooden planking. The sides of cupboards, cabinets and chairs were all constructed of woven oak scrub. Bent-grass turns up in the form of pleated saddle-pads, chair seats and horse collars. There are fine pieces of domestic horn implements in the shape of spoons, ladles and drinking cups. The manufacture of these horn articles was largely a tinker's trade, the secrets of which these itinerant people kept to themselves. There is also a complete set of the pearl-fisher's implements, including the claspstick and glass-bottomed flask which the tinkers used when searching the Spey for its pearl shells.

A point which strikes one forcibly when examining the goods and chattels of our forebears is that light was both extremely precious and usually very weak. Windows were only partially glazed. Lamps were of the crudest sort. Cruisie lamps and tallow candles, with a frequent resort to fir-wood splinters, provided the only means of illumination in many a Highland bothy. However, when few people could read, a dim light was in itself sufficient to weave, knot or whittle by.

The great dependence of the sparse population on the wild life of the country to provide them with the necessities of life is well demonstrated in this museum by a fine collection of the instruments of the hunter and fisherman. Many of these devices would today be regarded as gadgets of the poacher, but in those days the average Highlander killed to eat and not for sport. Foxes were killed for their skins, and possibly eaten. The fox traps shown are crude instruments; some of them look huge enough to hold a horse. Iron was scarce, and when available it was not infrequently of an inferior quality. The blacksmith had to make his engines of destruction big and strong so as to hold their victims.

For the angler there is much of interest in Am Fasgadh. A panel of salmon flies, perfectly preserved, shows that the fisher of old believed in colour and size. Some of these enormous lures must have proved more effective against the pike of the various Scottish lochs than the salmon of Spey and its many tributaries. Fish spears, reminiscent of those depicted in many an illustration of both Neptune and Britannia, adorn one wall of the sporting gallery. Braziers of iron with which the waters were burnt for salmon are on show. Such instruments, in the late eighteenth and the early nineteenth centuries, were considered devastating devices with which to lure these fish to their destruction; but in effect they are almost sporting implements when compared to the chemical warfare which the modern poacher employs against the salmon.

There is an unusual sporran made from the head-skin of a fine pine marten. Even in those days the capture of a marten must have been an uncommon event. Today the species in Scotland is rare indeed, although there is some evidence that *Martes martes* is on the increase in limited areas.

A pinchbeck, golden crown, is on view, which was worn by the owner of the champion cock at the annual contests which used to be run by the dominie, or schoolmaster, amongst his scholars in many a Highland parish. In the past cockfighting was a popular sporting pastime amongst the scattered Highland communities.

There is so much of interest within the walls of this most unusual museum that it would require a catalogue of considerable bulk to describe all its contents. A personal visit is the only real practical solution. Should you be interested in agriculture and its history, there is a fine big barn at the back of the house which contains a remarkable assembly of the tools and implements which were once used by those who sought a living from the soil.

EDGAR HOLLOWAY

ROSS AND CROMARTY

MORAY FIRTH

Lossiemouth
Spey Mouth
Loch Spynie
Invergordon
Cromarty
CROMARTY FIRTH
Findhorn
Elgin
Portgordon
Fochabers
Dingwall
Nairn
Forres
INVERNESS FIRTH
MORAY
BEAULY FIRTH
Arndilly
Inverness
NAIRN
Craigellachie
R. Spey
BANFF
Lochindorb
LOCH NESS
R. Spey
Grantown
N
Nethybridge
Lethendry Voil
Abernethy Forest
Kinveachy
L. Garten
Tulloch
MONADHLIATH MOUNTAINS
Aviemore
Craigellachie
Coylumbridge
Revoan
STRATHSPEY HOTEL
Glenmore
Mam Suim
INVERNESS
KENNEPOLE HILL
Ord Ban
Lo
Morlich
Ski-lift
Kinrara
Rothiemurchus
Forest
Cairn Gorm Mountains
Kincraig
Invereshie
Loch an Eilean
SUMMIT 4,084
Corrie Buidh
THE LURCHER
Larig Ghru
POOLS OF DEE
Kingussie
Am Fasgadh
Sgòr an Dubh Mor
Bothy
Ben Macdhui
Newtonmore
Glen Finich
Ruthven
L. Einich
Braeriach
Corrieyairack Forest
Cairn Toul
R. Spey
Laggan Br.
ABERDEEN
L. Spey
Glen Feshie
County Boundaries
Main Roads
Glen Feshie Forest
Balmoral Forest
0 1 2 3 4 5 6 7 8 9 10
Miles
Dalwhinnie
Glen Ey Forest